CUMBERSOME CORPSE

CUMBERSOME CORPSE

True Stories of Murderers Who Couldn't Get Rid of the Body

BRUCE SANDERS

BARNES
&NOBLE
BOOKS
NEW YORK

1995 Barnes & Noble Books

ISBN 1-56619-935-2

Printed and bound in the United States of America

M 9 8 7 6 5 4 3 2 1

For M.V.D. in retirement
and because he understands
that blood is sometimes
accompanied by thunder

CONTENTS

FOREWORD

Iᴛ is a demonstrable fact that most destroyers of a fellow human being who afterward seek to conceal effectively the physical evidence of their murderous folly, lack of emotional or mental control, overweening greed, lust, or outright fear are men.

Very few women who slay seek to conceal the corpse for which they are responsible unless they have an active masculine partner in the crime and its concealment. This also is a demonstrable fact.

Which makes one of the cases included in this collection particularly unique, for it relates how a mother and her daughter undertook to dispose of a particularly gruesome body by dispatching it on a journey to a destination where no one was expecting it.

The other eleven cases relate killings by violent males who employed strangulation by rope or bare hands or both, a blunt weapon, a gun, poison, a sharp weapon, or occasionally an assortment of these means of destruction. Afterwards they sought to walk away from their guilt.

To make this practicable they variously tried consuming their victim by flame, burial on enclosed premises or in some isolated pastoral setting with or without the aid of lime, mutilation and piecemeal disposal, dropping the victim down a well or taking it up a steeple, formal burial at a very early hour in a churchyard, storage in a depository, or dispatch by rail.

9

Some performed more than once, for in crime as in most other human pursuits success breeds confidence and frequently makes for repetition, and a repeat performance has a way of providing its own *cachet* for the performer.

All twelve, it must be admitted, have little in common apart from the salutary fact that their crime was discovered, and afterwards their perpetrators' identities were established and their sordid secret histories made horribly public. At least two destroyed themselves and one was committed to an asylum, while another was sufficiently theatrical, howbeit unwillingly, to die of a heart attack under a shower of money he had just removed from a bank without any bank officer's approval or consent.

But they are each and all terribly and absorbingly fascinating, not only for what they achieved with horrifying success, but for the dramatic quality of their several failures. In every case this proved to be a much more strenuous and demanding exercise than the mere act of brutal slaughter—which of course is why they failed and why their grim sagas can be told here.

The selection of the cases chosen for inclusion was for the most part achieved by the omission of such similar performers whose stories are perhaps currently too well known to justify repetition here.

These included Christie, Field and Gray, Crippen, Mahon, Robinson, Landru, Petiot, Haigh, Hume, Wainwright, H. H. Holmes, and that ogre Sheward who could have given points to Mahon but might have learned something from several of the performers in this collection.

✴ 1 ✴

The Case of the Fiery Bluff

SHORTLY after the close of the First World War a man aged about thirty stepped into a doctor's waiting-room in Berkeley, California, and told the receptionist he had come for a check-up. She wrote down his name, Charles Henry Schwartz. She also noted that he was good-looking, smiled easily, and wore his clothes well.

In the consulting room, when his new patient had taken off his shirt, the doctor saw a curious scar on the well-muscled chest.

"How did you come by this, Mr. Schwartz?" he inquired.

"I flew in the French Air Force during the war," his caller told him. "I had a lot of luck, but one day I'd used up my ration. That German bullet put me in hospital for months. At that, doc, I was still in luck, I guess, to come out on my own two feet."

Schwartz laughed with a kind of modest embarrassment. To the doctor, who found himself warming to his new patient, he appeared a likeable and even charming young man.

While his fingers probed and tapped healthy flesh he inquired if his patient intended to settle in Berkeley.

"I intend to set up an experimental laboratory at Walnut Creek," he was told. "Pure luck, doc, but I accidentally discovered a new scientific process that will revolutionize——"

The enthusiastic young man caught himself up and gave another short laugh. "Well, never mind what it will do. It needs
perfecting, and that'll take a lot of work, but when I'm through
you'll hear about it. The whole world will hear about it."

The doctor was impressed. He told his friends about the
newcomer and his programme. When the laboratory was
opened in an old building out at Walnut Creek, beyond the
Berkeley town limits, a good many people expected to hear one
day that young Mr. Schwartz had achieved the perfection for
his process that he sought.

But the months passed into years, and the newcomer became
accepted as a solid citizen, and when he married and later
became a father few bothered about his process or what it
would revolutionize. Charlie Schwartz was a pleasant man,
good company, and he paid his way. That was enough.

By 1925 he was thirty-six, still better-looking than the
average man, and he was the father of three children. His
friends were occasionally dropped hints about his process and
the development of his latest experiments. Schwartz was a
chemist who spoke German fluently. He had worked with a firm
of chemical manufacturers, but had always been interested in
trying out his own theories in practical bench work with
bunsen burners and retorts, chemicals and reagents. It was
believed by his friends that it was when engaged on such an
experiment he had discovered how to make artificial silk of
better quality than generally supplied by manufacturers and
at a lower cost than commercial rayon, which was the monopoly
of vast firms with world-wide markets.

Schwartz had claimed that his process was different from
any in commercial use, and technically it was vastly superior.
However, there were some sceptics when time passed without
the laboratory at Walnut Creek producing a perfected process
which would make its discoverer famous, and these hinted at
Schwartz being a big talker whose actions failed to measure up
to his words. Few listened to them. Schwartz was liked for his

geniality and bonhomie, and a man who is genuinely liked is usually accorded loyalty by his friends.

In 1924 a very different person arrived in Berkeley.

His name was Gilbert Warren Barbe. He had no good looks and he didn't make friends easily. In fact, most persons shied from him, for Barbe was a missionary. He believed fervidly that he had seen the Light. After serving with the American troops in the Ardennes slaughter he had returned to the United States a disillusioned and embittered young man, who saw no purpose to human existence. With his faith in himself and his fellows at very low ebb the Light appeared, and he knew what he must do.

He must set out on a crusade. He must tramp clear across the United States, carrying the true Christian message, bringing the Light he had seen into other men's lives. The young evangelist lived frugally. He endured physical hardship at times, but as cheerfully as he endured the jeers and contumely of the ribald mob that often assembled to listen to his brotherly message. Gil Barbe was a zealot, and his zeal wore down the jibes of the mockers. When the police moved him on he offered neither resistance nor complaint. He wore his cheerfulness like a badge.

When he brought it to Berkeley the first stage of his missionary tour had been completed. He decided to settle down for a while and take stock of his life. He arrived at an old derelict shed on the outskirts of the town and set about making it his home. Passers-by looked upon him as a hobo, and a few voiced the fear that he might be starting a hobo jungle, but any who stopped to talk to him came away impressed with his friendliness and pleasant though simple personality. He was not well read except in certain books of the Bible, and he was no rational debater. But he was obviously a young man who believed the simple gospel he preached, and his very lack of subtlety made him acceptable to many who might otherwise have been critical.

So Gil Barbe was tolerated. "A cranky guy with no real harm in him," was the verdict of most who met him.

One of those was the married chemist who had still to announce to the world that he could commercially manufacture artificial silk of better quality and more cheaply than anyone else.

Surprisingly the two men, of such very different outlooks, living in wide-apart social strata, became close friends. Gil Barbe evinced an interest in chemistry although he had no practical experience of laboratory work. Schwartz, the family man, listened attentively to the articles of a simple faith expounded by a man who had willingly devoted his life to following in the steps of the Nazarene and preaching the Christian ethic.

The two such dissimilar friends met mostly at the shack which the monkish missionary considered his home. They spent long hours together in the early summer of 1925. The coming of Schwartz was always welcomed by the man whose private life was patterned to the simplicity of a hermit's.

Undoubtedly Gil Barbe heard about Schwartz's hopes for his process. The two men probably discussed aspects of the experiments Schwartz said he was currently conducting. He may even have gone to the Walnut Creek laboratory and had the process explained.

He certainly told no one of going to Walnut Creek. Nor did he tell anyone that he intended to continue his active mission and leave for another part of the country. Which made it all the more surprising when in July he disappeared.

He was not seen washing his few culinary vessels outside his shack. At night no candlelight gleamed through the cracks and chinks in the lopsided weather boarding. Passers-by made comment on his disappearance.

"You seen that hobo around?"

"No, come to think of it I haven't. Probably started off on his travels again."

That was good for a light laugh, not necessarily tinged with malice, for now he had gone people surprisingly found they remembered the gentle Gil Barbe with a tolerance that surprised themselves.

But he had made no real impact on their lives. They quickly forgot him. Indeed, he had done little by which to be remembered, and the advent of a new model Ford was really a subject for enthusiastic gossip.

A hot July burned away.

Schwartz became engrossed in another round of his endless experiments at his Walnut Creek laboratory. He went early and remained late, apparently utterly absorbed in the outcome of the new tests. The Mexican night watchman arrived at seven o'clock in the evening of the 30th, accompanied by his dog. He heated some soup and took a bowl of it to his employer, working in a room at the head of a flight of stairs. The door was locked and he banged on it with his clenched fist.

It opened and Schwartz stood in the opening. He looked like a man with troubles trying to appear normal.

"Hello, Gonzalez," he said. "A hot night. Thanks for the soup. I'll let it cool."

He took the bowl from the Mexican's hands. As he did so the watchman's dog gave a curious howl. It was prancing around the closed door of a cupboard set under the stairs.

Schwartz swore, put down the soup, and ran down the stairs cursing the dog. The animal continued growling at the closed door, and Schwartz kicked it away.

"Get out," he yelled.

Yelping with hurt surprise, the dog ran outside the building as Gonzalez came clattering down the stairs.

"What's the matter, Mr. Schwartz?" he asked. "That dog don't mean any harm. There was no need to kick him."

The Mexican sounded offended, and Schwartz at once became apologetic.

"I'm sorry, Gonzalez," he said. "I think I've been overworking. It's my nerves. Here, I'd like you to do me a favour."

He took some money from his pocket and handed it to the staring Mexican.

"Go into town, Gonzalez. Buy me an alarm clock at a drug store, and bring me back some chewing gum. You'll do that?"

"You mean right now?" the Mexican inquired.

"Choose your own time," he was told. "No need to hurry. Too hot for that." Schwartz glanced up the stairs. "Guess that soup's cool enough by now."

He left Gonzalez standing with the money in his hand and returned up the stairs.The night watchman heard the door close, the key in the lock turn, and went out to find his scared dog. Then he started for the nearest shops, made the purchase Schwartz wanted, and started back for the laboratory.

When he arrived he left the dog outside, entered, and climbed the stairs. Schwartz was scowling when he opened the locked door.

"Back already!" he exclaimed in what seemed to the Mexican to be an irritated voice. "You better take the rest of the night off. No need for you to hang around while I'm here and I don't want to be interrupted any more."

Gonzalez nodded, took his dismissal with a shrug, and again clamped down the stairs and outside the laboratory. It was a few minutes to nine o'clock.

About a quarter of an hour later Schwartz rang his home. His wife answered the call, and she thought he sounded tired when he said, "I'm finishing for the night. I'll be leaving in a few minutes and I'll come straight home."

Mrs. Schwartz sat down to await her husband's home-coming. He never arrived. The next morning the reason was printed in the daily newspaper under a large headline. The reporter who covered the holocaust wrote:

"So great was the concussion that it seemed as if a war-time bomb had exploded, shattering windows and dishes in nearby houses, and frightening residents within a wide area. Red flames shot high in the sky after the blast, and the laboratory became a raging inferno."

It was not high-class reporting, but the story was big news locally. Schwartz's Walnut Creek laboratory had been gutted by fire following an explosion, and the chemist who had phoned his wife he was about to leave and come straight home was missing.

Police and firemen toiled at clearing the charred ruins of the building where Schwartz had spent so many hours. They came upon what the flames had left of a man. The conclusion was easily jumped at by most people without any effort at accepting credibility.

Something had gone amiss in Schwartz's last experiment. The explosion had occurred as he was on the point of clearing up for the night, and cruel disaster had overwhelmed the man and his secret process.

Guy Spencer was the Berkeley fire chief. He was a cautious man who looked long and hard at things before accepting their face value. He turned his professional eye on the laboratory ruins and started to trace the apparent course the flames had taken. He decided the fire had not been the outcome of an accident. It had been started deliberately.

Either Schwartz had been murdered or the chemist had committed suicide. He went back to the wrecked building with detectives and pointed out the charred work bench where Schwartz might have been when the explosion shattered the July night. He pointed to a half-dozen rudely contrived torches or flares made from cloth wrapped around sticks. They had been soaked in an inflammable liquid. From their condition he argued that they had been touched off separately, but the cases of stacked explosive against a party wall had not been set off, as apparently had been the wrecker's intention. Had all the explosives gone up the entire building would have been levelled. No charred shell would have remained standing, and it would have been impossible to say what had happened with certainty.

Guy Spencer, however, was very certain of his views. A stout brick wall and some heavy pieces of machinery had by a fluke kept the flames from reaching the stacked explosives. Even so the brick wall would have collapsed had not his men arrived in time.

Someone had miscalculated.

The police decided the fire chief had dumped a case of murder in their laps. A killer had disposed of Charles Henry Schwartz by wrecking his laboratory building, and had hoped to destroy the body of the victim completely beyond recognition in the blaze following the explosion.

But what motive could the killer have? That was where the police dragged their feet. Schwartz was a man everyone liked and so far as inquiry revealed had no enemies.

The initial police inquiry took several days. Mrs. Schwartz formally identified the grim remains of the victim as her husband's. A shocked Gonzalez told his story and supported the widow's identification.

The Berkeley police chief telephoned Dr. E. O. Heinrich, a noted criminologist and a professor at the University of California. He was formally asked to give his assistance on the case. Few scientists in the United States, appealed to by police departments, equalled the performances of Professor Heinrich in the field of forensic science. He set standards which are still accepted today, and he was one of the back-room experts in criminal investigation who became a legend in his own lifetime and won international fame.

The human remains found in the gutted building were sent to San Francisco, where they were examined and photographed and X-rayed. Then they were put in deep freeze.

Heinrich studied the X-ray photos and admitted they appeared to support the formal identification of Mrs. Schwartz and the Mexican. But his study of the other photos could not lead him to decide whether the dead man had been placed where he was found or had dropped there while trying to escape the flames. The flames had burned too much away from the charred frame.

However, Heinrich had a question. If the intention had been to blow up the entire building, as the stacked explosive suggested, why had the victim's remains been found in the position in which they had been lying? This seemed to suggest a killer's plan had gone awry. Encouraged by the eminent scientist's cautious views, the Berkeley police began fresh inquiries, and learned of a youth named Gallagher. He lived near the wrecked laboratory, and on the night of the explosion ran to the scene when the flames were shooting skyward. On his way to the fire he had to jump aside to avoid a car speeding towards him without lights.

"I didn't see it clearly, because it was beginning to get dark," he told detectives. "But I had the impression the car was Mr. Schwartz's."

"You know his car?"

"Sure," he agreed, "I've seen it lots of times."

Someone who had picked up two hats near the gutted building on the day after the fire took them to the police. One was stained and caked with dried mud, and there was cellulose on the band. This was established as a hat that had belonged to Schwartz. No one recognized the second, which was discoloured, obviously had been worn a long time, and was stained with a caustic chemical. The most that could be said about this hat was that it might have been brown felt originally and the property of Schwartz's killer.

Mrs. Esther Hatfield, who had done secretarial work for Schwartz, went on record with a formal statement that lifted a few brows. In it she said:

"Mr. Schwartz always had a restless, nervous air, but

that day he seemed more than usually disturbed and uneasy. He paced the floor continuously, wiping sweat from the palms of his hands. Of course, it was hot, but I noticed that his eyes seemed to have a wild stare. Frequently he glanced at the small cupboard under the stairs when he left the laboratory. He had always been somewhat secretive about it, and no one knew what it contained. It was kept locked, and only he had a key to it."

Walter Gonzalez told his story of his dog's interest in the locked stair cupboard, and Schwartz's apparent alarm. Mrs. Schwartz was questioned about the cupboard, but she admitted that her husband had told her nothing about his work at the laboratory and she had not been encouraged to go there.

But she had news for the police when she phoned them to say her home had been burgled the previous night. Detectives found that the intruder had climbed the back porch and entered by the window of a spare bedroom. All he had taken were photos of Charles Henry Schwartz. Mrs. Schwartz was left with no photograph of her late husband.

Heinrich was informed.

"You must get a photo of Schwartz," he told the police, and when one was obtained from a friend of the chemist Heinrich took it to the San Francisco morgue, where he compared it with the remains taken from deep freeze. The right ear of the fire victim had not been entirely destroyed, and Heinrich saw that the lobe had been of the type known as Darwinian. However, the photo he had been given showed a right ear of very different shape.

The dead man's chest had been so charred that it was not possible to trace the scar mentioned by Dr. Barber when questioned by the police. The doctor had also told them that Schwartz's teeth had appeared sound, but a couple had been extracted from the upper jaw.

The teeth of the victim certainly revealed two similar

extractions from the upper jaw, but the majority of the remaining teeth were in very bad condition, some broken, others decayed. Heinrich examined the ruin of a mouth very closely and discovered that the two teeth missing from the upper jaw had been removed only a short while before. The gums remained swollen even in death, and the heat of the fire had not changed the raw linings of the cavities. Moreover, the remaining teeth were in positions suggesting the pressure of them had not been relieved long enough to change their normal angles.

Heinrich left the San Francisco morgue convinced that the remains he had examined were not those of Charles Henry Schwartz. Some unknown had been murdered, and the explosion and fire at the laboratory were truly a fiery bluff.

He had further supporting evidence. Before having the corpse returned to its deep freeze compartment he had examined the rest of the head and concluded that a fracture at the base of the skull had been caused by a heavy blow from a blunt weapon. Moreover, he had also decided that the burns on the body were not all of the same kind. Some were unquestionably the result of action by the flames, but others, he was satisfied, were the result of chemical heat, especially those on the hands, which appeared to have been subjected to the corrosive action of an undiluted acid. The reason was obvious. The killer had sought to destroy the victim's fingerprints. He had gone back to the head again, and by minute examination established that the missing eyeballs had been clumsily removed by someone with no surgical skill. Again, there could be only one reason. The victim's eyes had been a different colour from his murderer's.

Heinrich sent a report to the Berkeley police. In it he stated categorically:

"This body has been worked on to hide its true identity. That is the answer to our problem. Cunning means, devilish means, have been used not only to destroy existing identification marks, but to manufacture new ones. All this mutilation was done deliberately and coolly by someone who first slew his victim by a blow on the back of the head."

The police were now confronted by the task of finding a murderer who had tried to lose his victim's body by substituting it for his own. The fiery bluff had not worked. Another perfect crime had fallen far short of perfection.

In death as well as life, it seemed, perfection had eluded Charles Henry Schwartz. To make sure by what margin it had eluded him Professor Heinrich visited the fire-blackened shambles at Walnut Creek. His findings there shocked a good many people who read about them.

"All bunkum," was how he described the laboratory.

It had no gas supply and water was not laid on. No serious research could have been done in a place as cold as an ice-house in winter, when the only illumination would have been provided by a paraffin lamp, hung on a bracket in one room to shine through the open door of the next. No artificial silk could have been manufactured in such surroundings.

"Then what's it all about?" a detective asked Heinrich.

"You could start looking for investors who parted with cash," Heinrich replied grimly. "They can probably tell you."

The Berkeley police extended their search for information about Schwartz's movements before the explosion. They found he had a short while before advertised for an assistant with small feet and hands. This odd requirement made sense when it was remembered Schwartz himself had small feet and slim tapering fingers. At this stage Walter Gonzalez was asked to jog his memory, and he recalled a man calling at the laboratory late one night in reply to the advertisement. A motorist named Benetis, who lived not far from Walnut Creek, remembered giving a lift one night to a man who told him he was on his way to a new job with what he called the Schwartz outfit.

A real job of clearing up the mess in the gutted laboratory was now undertaken, and Heinrich returned to it and made a fresh examination of the premises. On a section of unscorched floor he found bloodstains. Others were found in the stair cupboard. He was convinced the victim had been slain in the crude workshop and the body stowed in the stair cupboard. When he sifted some of the cleared debris he came upon pages of religious literature. Under his microscope the scorched pages revealed some of the text of a small edition of the New Testament, as well as pages from two pamphlets. One was entitled *John the Apostle*, the other had the challenging title of *The Philosophy of Eternal Brotherhood*. It was on the crisp brown flyleaf of the first that Heinrich picked out some spidery handwriting. By treating that page to various chemical tests he was able to bring up the name G. W. Barbe, followed by names of towns in Texas, with a date against each.

It didn't take the Texas police very long to report that an evangelist named Gilbert Warren Barbe had stayed in those towns and left on the dates given.

Heinrich had found the true identity of the victim. There was no reason why the fearful remains of a lover of his fellow-men should not now be given Christian burial, so all that was human of Gilbert Warren Barbe was interred in a cemetery at Martinez. By which time a hue and cry for Charles Henry Schwartz had been extended throughout the entire United States. Investigating detectives found that the man they sought had at different times employed various aliases. He had been known as Leon Henry Schwartzhoff, and as John Doe Stein, a character with a reputation for playing very fast and very loose with easily misled females. The police description of the wanted fugitive stressed that he had a trick of jingling coins in his pocket, smoked brown cheroots, and walked with a very straight back.

Reporters had a field day. They came up with the startling news that not long before the explosion the popular and hail-fellow-well-met Schwartz had scraped an acquaintance with Captain Lee of the Berkeley police, with whom he had discussed how the police department functioned when hunting a murderer. He had pumped Captain Lee on the subject of the perfect murder, only to be told the policeman's frank opinion.

"There's no such thing except in fiction."

It must have been terribly disconcerting. But it had not deterred a determined killer. So there must have been a pressing reason for both murder and flight. Motive was uncovered when inquiries established that Schwartz had insured his life against an industrial explosion for two hundred thousand dollars, the equivalent of about a million today.

The breaking up of the public image of the likeable, friendly Charles Henry Schwartz continued with almost cruel regularity. His alleged secret process was found in a notebook. It had been copied from a textbook for manufacturing chemists. Some artificial silk he had shown acquaintances interested in putting up money for research had been purchased at a store for eight dollars. The Army checked back on its hero and found he had never been a flying ace in the French or any other air force. He had been a member of a Red Cross unit transferred to the artillery after claiming engineering experience. The charlatan had finished the war as company barber.

Days passed, with interest in the manhunt increasing rather than abating, and one morning two strangers called on Captain Clarence D. Lee of the Berkeley police. One was a C. W. Hayward, from Oakland, the other his friend N. B. Edmunds, who lived in Berkeley. Hayward explained that he had recently let a room in his apartment house at Forty-first Street to a Harold Warren, who had paid a month's rent in advance and kept very much to himself. But once he had discussed the laboratory mystery with his landlord, and had admitted to some knowledge of chemistry as well as insisting that of course the body found was that of the chemist who had rented the place.

The Oakland police were contacted by Captain Lee. A raid

was planned without publicity, and a plain-clothes man arrived outside Harold Warren's door and rapped on it.

"Police," he shouted, banging again. "Open up."

There was no sound from the far side of the locked door. The plain-clothes man stood back and other detectives threw themselves at the door. As they did so a shot rang out. When the police burst into the room they found Schwartz lying across an unmade bed. A gun was held in his right hand. He was dead.

It had been a close thing. On the table was a packed suitcase and a roll of currency. In a pocket of the suicide's jacket was a letter addressed to his wife containing a confession and begging her forgiveness for how he had treated her in the past.

The plea had meaning when the unhappy woman confided to Captain Lee that her husband had squandered her modest fortune, and after his burial her total resources were less than the six hundred dollars found in the room in the Oakland apartment house.

Lee was satisfied she had been no accessory to murder. Schwartz had planned on her ignorance and innocence helping to ensure the insurance money was paid to her. He would have remained in hiding until it was safe to rejoin her, when he would probably have persuaded her to go abroad with him, possibly to some country with no extradition arrangement with the United States. There her usefulness would have been at an end, and he would have felt free to continue an earlier philandering role.

However that might be, the chances were on Schwartz successfully losing Gil Barbe's body had not Professor Heinrich insisted on being supplied with a photo of a man who had planned a fiery bluff that failed when the likeness was found and given to the famous criminologist.

The Case of the Temple's Secret

T HE young Frenchman with the brooding eyes and weak mouth stared at the work he had completed in the room where August sunshine splashed the walls. In that same room scraps of history had been made in the days when the Du Barry told her interior decorator to cover those walls with a dusky rose tint that she was to make famous.

The brooding young man with the dark hair riding up from his scalp was himself an interior decorator, employed by a maker of radio and television sets to beautify these rooms designed for the roseate mistress of the lecherous Louis XV. He had thought himself inspired in his work when love touched his life. Now he had lost his assurance.

He had seen his love for something else and had found fear. Fear of his parents, fear of where he was drifting, fear of the Englishwoman who was three years younger than himself and had awakened his dormant desire and fired his dreams. Too much fear, in fact, for him to live with.

The dreams had burned to cold ash, and desire had lost its warmth when its novelty had palled in satiety and a cold worm of repugnance had eaten holes in his conscience.

He glanced at his watch.

At eleven o'clock that Sunday morning he had a rendezvous with the English nurse who had become his mistress. Nine days previously she had returned from England. She had no job to go back to, and was staying at a cheap little hotel in Paris called the Hôtel de Londres. She had returned to France as a result of their discussion when he visited her in England. She wanted the two things most women wanted from a lover, marriage and a home.

It would have been simpler if he had told her the truth while in England—that he was tired of her, that their grand passion was in reality a drab little escapade in lust. But in England he had been alone and a coward.

Now he was still a coward, but he was not alone. There was his family. He felt fortified and comforted and resolved.

He walked out of the sunlit room, careful to attract no attention from the staff employed by Monsieur Greyfier de Bellecombe in his sumptious Château du Barry, and out into the park-like grounds, where birds shrilled in the leafy summer trees and a girl with eager lips and bright blonde hair would meet him with a burnished query in her blue-grey eyes. He felt as though he was turning his back on all he had lived through up to that strange moment of challenge, and the feeling had a haunting quality. His mind was confused. He tried to think of the lunch he had planned to share with Jacky at the Bon Gîte restaurant, but found difficulty in concentrating.

Breathing heavily, he hurried his steps. He left the stone-flagged path and struck off across the park's greensward, thankful that Monsieur Dallongeville, who had charge of the château grounds, was absent on his annual holiday, like the Bellecombe family.

It should not take Jacqueline Richardson long to come the twelve miles or so from Paris, and he was sure she would not be late.

Actually she was early.

She was waiting for him with her eager smile and open arms when he came to the place of rendezvous.

"Oh, Jean," she said, "it's seemed such a long time. And

now we're together again." There was tenderness in her glance, but it concealed a heat that could burst into flame. "Let's go to the temple. It'll be like old times."

The reminder had a knife edge. She was referring to the days when they first found love, when he was working at the château and the English nurse was minding the younger members of the Bellecombe family. Those days when they wandered hand in hand up the grassy knoll to the little circular Temple of Love, with its eight pillars and balcony arranged like a coronet in masonry that had shared the secrets whispered by the Du Barry in a royal embrace. Not that the young interior decorator was sparing much thought for a dissolute Bourbon and his mistress as he caught the English girl's plump arm.

"I think we'll go for a walk, Jacky. Afterwards we can have lunch at the Bon Gîte."

"I want to go to the temple, Jean."

They went to the temple, where the quarrel began like a summer storm. The recriminations came fast, followed by the accusations and impossible threats.

For the English girl was suddenly afraid of losing the man to whom she had given herself freely, this man whom she had assured herself was the only man she wanted to marry.

The Frenchman became scared of her shrill demands and the almost hysterical threats accompanying them.

He thought desperately of his parents, his job and its prospects, and a future that was hidden by a haze of doubt.

"We're finished, Jacky. I've got to tell you."

When the words were spoken he felt a vast relief, and something that could have been shame, but his emotions just then were too mixed to be readily analysed.

She smacked his face, and her hand was heavy.

"Never, Jean. You're not leaving me."

Angered, trembling with fear for what she might do to his life, he picked up a piece of wood. She screamed—once. Then the stick he wielded as a club smashed against the blonde head. She fell in the shadow of the Temple of Love, and he tossed the stick away into the dark undergrowth. She stirred, and he knelt and caught up her pale head, the shining hair streaked with bright fresh blood.

His long tapering fingers, which he had been told belonged to an artist, closed convulsively around her throat, and he knew only a desire to punish her, to make her suffer.

The grasp of the slim fingers tightened. He held his breath. When he slowly removed his hooked hands the girl he had once thought he loved lay dead, her face not pretty. He lifted one of her hands and watched the scarlet drops of the fingernails fall as he released it. He crouched there, staring at her, his eyes shocked into deeper brooding than before.

At the groundsman's shed he would find a spade. For he must hide the body.

He rose and turned his back on the sprawled limbs of the dead girl. On the point of walking away, he turned back and removed her shoes. He stuffed one into each of his pockets.

Then he noticed her handbag. He picked it up and opened it. Inside he found two thousand francs, then worth about two pounds, which he removed and pocketed.

As he turned away again he was concentrating on the spade.

On a bitterly cold February day in 1953 two wood-cutters tramped among the bare trees below the knoll on which the Du Barry's Temple of Love was reared like a gigantic but very stale wedding cake. A north-east wind whistled among the pillars. The two men began clearing the ground and the elder, whose name was Davoust, was attracted by a sudden shout from his companion, Dauvergne.

"Hey. I've found a body."

The younger man was scratching away the soil and frozen clods and leaves from a shallow trench he had discovered. A tangle of matted undergrowth almost covered the place, and he had pushed this aside when clearing the ground, so coming upon the trench and its contents.

The young girl had been dead for months, but her blonde hair still shone like mirrored silk.

Charles Davoust of Louveciennes and young Lucien Dauvergne of Vaucresson hurried to inform their foreman, Jean Morin, of their find. There was no more forestry that day in the park of the Du Barry's château. The police took over. Commissaire Vasseur and the Sûreté's Premier Brigade Mobile began an investigation that was long overdue.

Overdue because months before that day the French police had received a communication from a Mrs. Lorraine Kent, living in London, inquiring the whereabouts of her friend Jacqueline Richardson, whom she had last heard from in August 1951 when she was staying at the Hôtel de Londres in Paris.

Had the French police, upon receipt of Mrs. Kent's inquiry, started to check up on the English nurse's whereabouts they must surely have approached the staff of the Château de Louveciennes, and then they would have heard of Jean Liger and his swift wooing. But it is a fact that has been pointed out more than once that the French police are curiously tardy in investigations concerning missing or murdered British nationals. Following the arrival of Mrs. Kent's letter in Paris, nothing was done that uncovered the amorous relationship between Jean Liger and his English mistress, a nurse employed at the château.

It was Lucien Dauvergne who lit a firecracker and dropped it under the chair-borne rumps of the Sûreté Nationale.

More than a year too late detectives arrived to begin asking questions at the château, and they very soon heard of Jacqueline Richardson, who had made no secret of her affection for an interior decorator, and of how she had suddenly left her employ. They dug out the inquiry from Mrs. Kent from a mound of dead dossiers, blew the dust off it, and set about making up for lost time. A *commission rogatoire* was sent to Scotland Yard, asking for information.

Lucien Dauvergne's grisly find in the Du Barry's park cleared a lot of international news from the front pages of Paris newspapers. Here was a *crime passionel* with a difference. That difference was a dead Englishwoman. She had died, according to police surgeons, from strangulation and death had come to her eighteen months before.

There was a welter of tantalizing details. Missing shoes and red-lacquered toenails, missing handbag and bright blonde hair with scabs of dried blood. There were also people at the château with background information. Reporters and photographers poured out of Paris and headed for the Château de Louveciennes, where the Du Barry was arrested by a yelling mob in the year of the Terror.

They learned what the château servants had told the police. The English nurse had been infatuated with the interior decorator. She had told some of the staff her wedding had been arranged. The couple were understood to be betrothed.

"We celebrated with champagne," one of the servants told the Paris reporters.

But there had been no marriage. The servants had become aware of a chill growing between the lovers. One day the English nurse packed her bag and left for England. Jean Liger avoided the staff. He had seemed unhappy and depressed. Then he too disappeared from the château. The strange lovers were forgotten until the young woodsman in the grounds scraped the covering off the shallow trench and revealed the temple's secret.

The case continued to make headlines in the Paris newspapers while Commissaire Vasseur and his team of detectives began a hunt for new clues and a young interior decorator.

They established that the Englishwoman had arrived back in Paris from London on July 27th, 1951. Monsieur Ribierre of the Hôtel de Londres told detectives he remembered Jacqueline Richardson very well.

"She was slim and *petite*," he explained. "She came to me and very frankly asked me to let her have my cheapest room. She had only a little money and had to go out and find a job to pay the rent."

He had given her the key to a room that cost only two hundred and fifty francs a night, about five shillings at that time.

Monsieur Ribierre also recalled August 5th, the day he last saw his English guest.

"I haven't seen her since that day," he explained. "I was surprised because later her bags and clothes were collected by someone else."

"Who was this person?" he was asked.

On that important point the hotel manager could not help the police.

But Jean Liger could.

Detectives had found him, and when approached had appeared nervous, but not distrait. For a young man capable of uncontrollable violence he had kept a surprising number of souvenirs of his strangled mistress. Her luggage was found stored in his bedroom. On its sides were the curious hieroglyphics in green chalk of the French customs officers. A shelf in the room held some of the dead woman's hats.

Liger made a formal statement. It was not notable for old-time French gallantry. He claimed that he had fallen in love with Jacqueline Richardson while they were employed together at the château, but he had found her terribly possessive. They had shared periods of intense affection alternating with occasions when they quarrelled bitterly. Finally the English nurse in a fit of pique had left her employ in France and returned to England.

In London she had obtained a post as receptionist in the Grosvenor Hotel, and she was still on the Victoria hotel's staff when Liger followed her and sought reconciliation. After a torrent of kisses and fresh avowals Liger returned to France, but only to travel back to London, where Jacky agreed to come back to Paris and join him so they could be married in France. She returned, bringing her former possessiveness, and suddenly he knew it had all been a terrible mistake.

He had arranged to meet her that fatal Sunday, August 5th, 1951, at Louveciennes. Their sudden quarrel had torn at his reason. He claimed she had attacked him, and he had found himself striking down this young woman he had so shortly before cherished. Then he had found himself kneeling beside her with his fingers clutched around her throat.

He was frank about taking the two thousand francs from her handbag, which with her shoes he had dropped down a drain. He went to Paris and collected her things from the hotel where she had stayed. He had taken some of her luggage to a railway station and deposited it at a left-luggage counter. He said he had found it impossible for him to return to his parents' home. So he had taken a room in a modest hotel near the Pont de Neuilly, on the western outskirts of the French capital.

He said he had thought of going to the police.

He had presumably had second thoughts which advised not going. But he made no point of this in his statement to the detectives. When he had finished it was a drab recital. The only dubious feature of the inquiry was the nature of the charge that could be brought against Liger since he had claimed the Englishwoman had attacked him.

However, she had no weapon. Only her scarlet-tinted nails, often used by rejected mistresses, judging by the lavish covers of the French novels draping the sides of Paris newsagents' kiosks and the windows of Paris bookshops.

The French police weighed up the evidence and charged Liger with manslaughter.

With this charge on the record, they set about arranging for the inevitable reconstruction of the crime that is standard

French procedure in such an investigation. The chief legal functionary attending the reconstruction was the examining magistrate for the Versailles district, which includes Louveciennes in its area. On a blustery and rather cold day in March 1953 a procession of men muffled in overcoats started out for the Du Barry's park and her Temple of Love that had suddenly claimed front-page notice in the world's Press.

Liger was one of the party. He walked in handcuffs and a couple of detectives kept close to him, one at each side, as he once more trod the familiar paths in the château grounds. He gave a pantomime demonstration of what he claimed had happened.

The hard-faced procession trudged up the grassy knoll, where the trees were painted with the first flush of spring. Frowning detectives moved as he pointed. Questions flowed from the examining magistrate.

Liger answered them in a flat dull monotone.

Another statement from him went on the record. In it he elaborated his previous description of events immediately after the strangling.

He said, "I bound her feet with a leather belt she was wearing, and afterwards I dragged her body into the undergrowth."

He paused, and the official shorthand writer waited expectantly. The prisoner moistened lips dried by the March wind and cleared his throat nervously.

He went on, "Then I returned to the château, where I found a spade. I went back to the body and started to dig a grave, but I had not the courage to go on with the job, so I decided to return to Paris, and left the body lying on the ground."

There was another tense pause while the prisoner ran hands over his thin face, up over his eyes and along his trim moustache. He gave the impression of a man having trouble in arranging his thoughts.

He dropped his hands and continued: "When I was back in Paris I slept in a hotel because I did not want to go home to my parents, as I was in a state of great nervousness. The next day I returned to the château, after having debated within myself all night whether I should give myself up to the police. When I arrived in the grounds I found Jacky's body just as I had left it. I finished the grave, put her body in, and covered it with soil."

The new statement was close to the first; there were no significant differences on which to question him.

He was asked to point out where he had found the stick with which he had knocked her down. He walked some distance from where he was standing, watched closely by the detectives, and appeared to search for a place by some thick undergrowth. He lifted his manacled hands, pointing.

"There."

The shallow grave had been covered with a tarpaulin. This was removed. The examining magistrate gestured to one of the plain-clothes men, and the prisoner was led to the trench he had dug. The magistrate moved round the grave and stood on the opposite side facing Liger.

The prisoner was wearing a look of strain, and appeared to be on the point of collapse. But he pulled himself together and forced himself to look down at the trench without flinching. The examining magistrate awaited the outcome of a simple test in psychology. He was disappointed. The bad moments passed with Liger maintaining silence. His eyes were wide, fixed in an unnatural stare, but his mouth remained compressed. The examining magistrate moved his feet.

"Tell me what you did with her shoes," he said sharply.

Liger's eyes narrowed. He spoke very softly. "I took them away and threw them down a drain on my way back to Paris." He added quickly, "But I've already told you I don't know why I did this. I still don't know."

The group around the empty grave were silent while the examining magistrate watched the prisoner. He asked some more questions, receiving familiar answers, and the reconstruction of the crime was finished. Jean Liger's arm was held by one of his guards, and he was taken back to jail. He had to wait three years before he was brought to trial.

In that dragging interval the French police had plenty of time and opportunity to complete their formidable dossier on the dead Englishwoman. By the time the last detail was written down the world had forgotten the man languishing in prison.

Jacqueline Richardson, who after the discovery of her corpse became Jacky to newspaper readers throughout France, was born at Ironbridge, in Shropshire. Her parents were of modest means and separated when she was only a few months old. She was brought up by her father, and remained a virtual stranger to two half-brothers. When she was seventeen she set out to fend for herself and live her own life.

She started earning her own living when she took a job as waitress in a café. Later she moved to Cambridge before going to London for a short holiday. While in the metropolis she secured a position in a Paddington hotel. But she had restive feet. She returned to the West Country and took a job in a Bath hotel. In her spare time she studied French. She had a limited ambition. She wanted to obtain a post as children's nurse with a French family. She saw that as an opportunity for travel and seeing foreigners and their different ways of life.

When she felt she was ready to make the change she left Bath and went to Paris. Gay Paree did not overwhelm her, for she was a self-possessed young woman with plenty of backbone, and it was not long before she secured a post that suited her, with the family owning the lovely park around the Château de Louveciennes. There she found happiness, took pleasure in her duties, and flung herself into the open arms of Jean Liger.

She had told most of her personal story to her friend Mrs. Kent, with whom Jacqueline stayed for a while when she returned from France.

It was not a great deal to take three years in uncovering, and it might appear to the unbiased onlooker that the French police were in no hurry to bring Jean Liger to account for his crime.

The trial opened at last in the same assize court at Versailles where Henri-Désiré Landru, the notorious "Bluebeard of Gambais," had been tried thirty years before for his incredible multiple murders of foolish and trusting women. The courtroom was packed, and remained so throughout the January and February days that passed before a verdict was reached. The murder of the members of the Drummond family in a lonely spot in the South of France had thrown its elongated shadow over this case, where again the victim was English. The crowd that turned up daily arrived expecting thrills and disclosures. Almost the only disclosures they heard were scraps of alleged evidence blackening the character of the dead Englishwoman.

The judge stated that the prisoner had been described by a close friend as "an atheist with existentialist tendencies." If Jean-Paul Sartre read that statement he must have been shocked. As were a good many readers of the case as reported in the British newspapers. Accustomed to British court procedure, they read with astonishment some of the statements the prisoner was allowed to make without any sort of challenge from the prosecution.

Relating how the tragic love affair had developed, Liger fully slanted his words to provide the impression he wished his listeners to receive.

"I was hungry," he told the court, "and wanted to eat. But she felt romantic. She was so very insistent. So I weakly gave in to her. But each time I wanted to go and eat she wanted me to cuddle her. Eventually I said I was going to leave. She slapped my face and ran away."

The prisoner apparently did not realize that he was destroying the myth of the Frenchman as the paramount lover, and replacing it with a rather tawdry picture of a gourmand who put his stomach before his heart.

He told the attentive court: "It all happened because I

became overwhelmed by my pent-up feelings against her. She wanted me to act like an animal instead of a well brought-up young man. I wanted to show her I was not at her beck and call."

It must be admitted he showed her, dramatically and terribly conclusively, and the showing did not reveal him as well brought-up even by existentialist standards.

The judge read aloud from what was described by French reporters as a Scotland Yard report.

"She had many love affairs," he announced in a silver-threaded voice. "Some ended in quarrels, with screaming, blows, and scandal."

The public prosecutor had a piece to add.

"There is no doubt that she acted very badly with a number of men in England," he said rather insistently. "At the age of sixteen she left home. At seventeen she was living with an American in Cambridge. For a while she was an inmate of a house of ill-fame, in the hope that she would find a husband there."

The prisoner found himself impelled to announce in a quivering voice, "She was not the kind of woman I wanted to be the mother of my children."

As some piece of mitigation the judge felt called upon to point out that French friends of the dead woman had described her as being "sweet, timid, and reserved."

But Maître Jean Reliquet really got down to cases when he claimed the dead woman was both a mythomaniac—that is, someone unable to recognize what constitutes the truth—and a nymphomaniac.

He held a sheaf of notes, which he consulted just before he stated: "She had few scruples, and had been involved in swindles and blackmail. She also became involved in an affair with an R.A.F. doctor, and also with a young undergraduate who was madly enamoured of 'the prettiest girl in Cambridge.' From both these men she obtained sums of money.

"A woman who knew her in England," he continued, "and has heard of this case, has written to the Prefect of Police in Paris saying that because of the girl's nervous condition no man could stay in love with her for very long. Whenever a man wanted to break away from her she began a campaign of threats and terrible scenes."

Such was the picture drawn in the Versailles court of the woman Liger had chased to England to be with, whose clothes and hats he had kept for eighteen months. But no one could avoid the fact that Jacqueline Richardson had been done to death. The public prosecutor called the killing sordid and cowardly and claimed Jean Liger had strangled his mistress in a desperate attempt to rid himself of the problem of marrying her. Liger's lack of will-power had prevented him from solving his problem by reasoned argument. He had flinched from the scene he knew would occur when he told his mistress the truth about his changed feelings for her.

A wrangle ensued between the prosecution, the judge, and the defence, after which Liger again gave evidence in cross-examination.

"Shortly after we met," he related, "I accompanied her to her hotel. As we stood in front of the door, she gave me to understand that if I wished to sleep with her she was agreeable. I was deeply shocked."

The judge felt called upon to remind him: "A few days later she became your mistress."

"I became her lover," was the prisoner's cautious amendment. "She wanted to marry me, but it was not for a home or children. Rather to have someone like me at her disposal. She thought of nothing else. I didn't want to marry a love machine."

Unfortunately he did not explain what he understood by love. Had he done so it might have been very illuminating, not least for the public prosecutor. The prisoner went on to inform the frowning judge that it was consideration for his parents that stopped him from going immediately to the police with a confession about what had happened at the Temple of Love. He did not want them to know their son was a killer.

The trial continued in a heavy-footed fashion until February 7th, 1955. By that time a host of witnesses had cóme, said their piece, and left. On that day the court delivered sentence.

Seven years imprisonment for manslaughter.

But the reputation of Jacqueline Richardson had been more savagely handled than her body. Quite a few persons must have left the Versailles court at the close of the case with a very unpleasant taste in their mouths.

★ 3 ★

The Case of the Mother's Dream

Breakfast in the Tombe household at Sydenham was usually a very placid meal, but its peacefulness was shattered when grey-haired Mrs. Tombe looked up from her plate suddenly and said in a choked voice, "I had that dream again last night, Gordon."

Her husband glanced up from his morning newspaper, startled, as well he might be. He knew to which dream his wife referred. In his opinion it was more of a nightmare, and although he understood that it was induced by worry for their son, he could not bring himself to put any credence in it. He was a clergyman, and his training and belief made him sceptical of the night visions that passed for dreams. But he was very concerned for his wife's peace of mind, and he felt that anything he could do to allay the anxiety causing such a dream should be done as a matter of urgency.

"I didn't want to tell you, Gordon," his wife confessed, "but it is something I must share. I feel something ought to be done about it." She paused before adding, "It was so vivid, and I remember each detail so distinctly, I'm scared. I think we should do something, tell someone."

He reached across the breakfast table and held one of her hands in his.

"The police, my dear?"

She met his level glance, bit her under lip, and nodded in a jerky, tense motion. "Yes. I've thought about it, Gordon. I think you should go to Scotland Yard. I really do."

She withdrew her hand, and her husband said, "Tell me what you dreamed last night, my dear?"

His wife took some moments to compose herself before she said, "Well, it wasn't quite the same last night. I saw Eric again, but this time he wasn't trying to tell me something. He was very still. He was dead."

When she hesitated her husband asked, "Do you know where he was?"

"Yes," she replied. "At the bottom of a well. I'm sure he's been murdered, Gordon. I've never been so sure of anything in my whole life."

The fierceness with which she uttered the last words brought a frown to the husband's face.

"Very well, my dear," he said calmly. "I will pay a visit to Scotland Yard and ask them to find Eric for us." He leaned back in his chair. "Perhaps then you won't have this dream worry you again."

This was the reason that took the Reverend Gordon Tombe, a priest of the Church of England, to Scotland Yard in the late summer of 1923. He made known his business and was shown into a room where he met a trim-looking man who looked more like his conception of a barrister than a detective.

"I am Superintendent Carlin, Mr. Tombe," said the soft-voiced man with the carefully knotted tie and very trim moustache. "How can I help you?"

Across the width of a table littered with papers the visitor from Sydenham told the Yard superintendent about his wife's recurring dream, in which her son appeared as though he wished to warn her about some disaster.

"And now, Mr. Carlin, she has seen him lying at the bottom of a well. She is convinced that is where his body will be found."

"At the bottom of a well?"

"Yes."

"Where does he live?"

"Well, he lived at Kenley until there was a fire. We haven't heard from him for some time."

"Is there a well on the property?" Carlin inquired.

The troubled face above the clerical collar moved slowly from side to side.

"I really don't know. Eric certainly never mentioned one to his mother or to me."

Carlin's fingers drummed on the table top for several seconds before he said, "Mr. Tombe, I think you'd better tell me all you know about your son's recent activities."

He was told how George Eric Gordon Tombe, the clergyman's son, had always been fond of horses and riding. During the recent war he had met a suave, smooth-talking character named Ernest Dyer who had won his attention by discussing his plans for opening some stables. The two men had remained friendly, and after they had been demobbed Dyer called on the younger man and told him he had heard of a stud farm in Surrey, not far from London, being up for sale.

Eric Tombe's mother and father had found little attraction in the proposition, but their son had accepted with enthusiasm the chance to become Dyer's partner. He helped to raise a total capital of five thousand pounds, the place was purchased, and Dyer the business man of the partnership promptly paid the first premium on an insurance of twelve thousand pounds.

The stud farm was situated in Kenley, and its previous owner, who sold it to Dyer, was Percy Woodland, a trainer who had moved to bigger things in his career. The new owners moved into their property, and almost at once Dyer revealed a surprising passion for cars, one which took him away from The Welcomes Stud Farm for lengthy spells, while the inexperienced Eric Tombe was left to battle alone with the problem of training horses.

Not surprisingly the partners found themselves out of agreement about their investment and their business interests. The venture was doomed to eventual failure. It could only be a question of time before young Tombe admitted the truth he did not wish to see clearly.

In April 1921 while Tombe was absent from the farm it was badly damaged by fire. Dyer had lost little time in putting in his claim to the insurance company, which sent an investigator to review the damaged property. They had refused to pay the claim. Tombe had expected his partner to sue, but Dyer had no stomach for pressing his claim in a court of law. The fire fiasco had been the beginning of the end for the curious partnership. A year passed in fruitless argument, and almost on the anniversary of the fire Dyer and Eric Tombe ended their association in a sad-starred venture. Dyer had left, and the clergyman had not heard from his son.

Another year had passed, and the missing Eric Tombe's mother started to have bad dreams about her son, in which he appeared to pass on a warning of some kind which she could not understand.

"Let me have the address of your son's bank, Mr. Tombe," Carlin said when the clergyman came to the end of his narrative, "and also the addresses of any friends of his known to you."

When he had written them down he rose and shook hands with the unhappy father. "If I have news you'll hear from me, Mr. Tombe," he promised.

The clergyman returned to Sydenham.

Carlin lost no time in contacting the manager of the West End bank where Eric Tombe had an account. He was provided with information that struck him as most significant. For instance, in April 1922 the missing Eric Tombe's current account held a useful balance of more than twenty-five hundred pounds. However, at the end of that same month a letter from him conveyed instructions for thirteen hundred and fifty pounds to be transferred to the bank's branch in Paris, with the request that arrangements be made for Ernest Dyer to draw on it with no limit. Dyer's specimen signature was enclosed with the request.

Eric Tombe's signature had not been questioned, and the instructions had been accepted. Throughout May and June Dyer had drawn on the Paris balance, and in July the West End branch received additional instructions to allow Dyer to draw on the balance remaining in London.

Carlin had the two letters containing instructions to the bank produced and he signed for them. Before he left the manager's office he had been told of something that had perturbed the bank's officials. Dyer had made a trip to the West Country and there overdrawn the Tombe account. He had been handing out cheques which could not be honoured.

Among the addresses left with Carlin by the missing Eric Tombe's father was one of a young woman who had been a friend of both partners in The Welcomes venture. He paid her a visit and was told she hadn't seen the younger man for a year and a half. She related an incident which had puzzled her at the time.

With a friend and the two stud farm partners she had agreed to a short holiday trip to Paris. It was the period when the Bright Young Things were making news, and it was considered fashionably fast to indulge in a brief nervous fling in Paris, which was coming out of the stupor induced by war-time conditions and long-range shelling. The quartet agreed to meet on April 25th and take the boat train. The two young women were on time, and Dyer arrived late and alone, but with a telegram he said Eric Tombe had sent him, apologizing for having to go overseas at very short notice.

So Paris was out.

What had puzzled the young woman interviewed by the Yard superintendent was not the calling off of the trip, but Eric Tombe's use of the word "overseas" in his telegram. He had apparently had to go to France. Whenever he had spoken to her he had always said France, and she couldn't remember him using the soldier's word "overseas." Somehow it struck her as a false note.

She told Carlin she hadn't seen Dyer for about nine months, when she had heard he was going to the north of England. She did not know where or why he was making the trip. Carlin had inquiries made, but could not learn of anyone seeing Dyer in London after going north. It was important to trace Dyer, for he was the only person with a first-hand story of where Eric Tombe had vanished. So Carlin had a general inquiry sent to police forces in the north of England.

The routine inquiry produced the story of a man calling himself Fitzsimmons. The report had been handed in by an Inspector Abbott, who had been on the trail of a number of worthless cheques. Fitzsimmons had been a free spender and had talked loud and long in bars and saloons along the Yorkshire coast. He had also put a few advertisements in local papers, advising men of the highest integrity to apply to him for details of employment with very bright prospects.

"Of the highest integrity" had been his own choice of words. Inspector Abbott decided a newcomer to the Yorkshire coastal resorts, who behaved as though it were midsummer in the last days of November, could bear investigation. Moreover, one detail of the advertisement for men of the highest integrity had roused the C.I.D. inspector's suspicions. Apparently the highest integrity was not enough. Each applicant was to be intervewed in person by Mr. Fitzsimmons, and the interview would take place only if the applicant was able to produce a cash deposit to establish his *bona fides*.

For a man who had been littering Yorkshire's broad acres with dud cheques the request for cash looked to the inspector like a desperate attempt to line lean pockets.

Abbott called on Fitzsimmons at the hotel in Scarborough where the advertiser was staying. A visit from the police obviously took Fitzsimmons by surprise. He appeared nonplussed, but agreed to take the C.I.D. inspector to his room, where they could talk.

He didn't reach his room. On the way Abbott saw Fitzsimmons sneak a hand to his pocket, and the C.I.D. inspector decided the other had some incriminating papers he wished to destroy, and threw himself on his companion.

The two men collided against the wall, fell to the ground struggling, and Abbott was suddenly checked by the sound of a gunshot and the man under him going limp.

Fitzsimmons had not been reaching for incriminating papers as the C.I.D. inspector supposed, but for a revolver. In the dead man's room Abbott came upon a gambler's eyeshade and a mask, some soldier's service medals, and a badge from a branch of the British Legion. The case in which he found these personal effects had the initials E.T. stencilled on the side. It also held nearly two hundred blank cheques, on which had been pencilled the name of Eric Gordon Tombe. To Abbott it looked as though the pencilled name had been traced, and was there to be inked over at leisure. Some items of a personal nature, the property of this Eric Gordon Tombe, were found in the bag.

Fitzsimmons had obviously been a crook, and Abbott was sure the name was bogus. He started his own inquiry, and learned that Fitzsimmons was actually a certain Ernest Dyer. He was wanted for passing out a stream of rubber cheques in the West Country, and was currently sought by the police in Gloucestershire and Herefordshire.

Carlin finished reading a curious record that appeared to end his own inquiry before it had properly begun. Dyer had come to the end of his tether. Carrying that revolver had been the last comfort of a desperate man.

But what of Eric Tombe?

Carlin decided it was time to visit The Welcomes at Kenley. He had not been unduly impressed by the story of the dream related by the clergyman's wife. In his line of business dreams were very much at a discount. Any detective prepared to admit himself impressed by one would be endangering his career.

But the fire at the stud farm, the refusal of an insurance company to pay up, and the desperate last resort of Ernest Dyer pointed to a sequence of events that might yield much to closer scrutiny. Especially at the stud farm, where the two men invested their money and where the fire took place.

Kenley, where the stud farm was situated, was a few miles south of Croydon, on the very fringe of Z Division of the Metropolitan Police. Since the substitution of the Greater London Council for the London County Council Kenley has become a part of London, but in the nineteen-twenties it was very much in the country.

Carlin arranged to be met by Detective-Inspector Hedges of Z Division, and the two men arrived at the ruins of The Welcomes on a bright September day in 1923 and had to cut back the weeds choking a five-barred gate leading to the property.

The place was utterly derelict. Paths were overgrown and choked, brickwork of outbuildings and stables was crumbling badly, and the charred remains of the badly damaged house smelled of decay and stale embers, with over all a pervasive odour of damp. When the police had forced entry into the locked ruin they found little for their trouble. The place had obviously not been lived in for many months. There was a small cottage on the property. They broke into this. Again they found nothing to explain why or when the property had been deserted.

Carlin tramped the limits of the farm, and came upon five wells or cess-pits. Suitable drainage had obviously been a problem.

"I'll want these pits examined, Hedges," Carlin told the divisional man.

Inspector Hedges appeared surprised.

"What do you expect to find, sir?" he asked, obviously puzzled by the request.

"I'm not sure."

Constables in gumboots and shirt-sleeves began clearing the vegetation and slabs of broken concrete from the first of the dried-up wells. By the time they had cleared two of the pits and assured Carlin they held nothing of interest for the Yard man the September day was dying.

"What do we do now, sir?" asked Hedges, aware that his men were tired after their exertions.

"Let the men rest, then start on number three," Carlin told him.

Hurricane lanterns were lit, and the heaving policemen began tearing away the weeds and knee-high grasses choking the mouth of the third well. When the weeds had been cleared they found more rubble blocking the pit.

Obviously someone had been careful to fill in all the pits, which seemed a curious waste of time, for it had been work that served no useful purpose except, perhaps, to discourage anyone from searching.

It was an eerie scene under the trees beyond the gutted farmhouse, where the lanterns threw long, wildly gyrating shadows over the ground and up among the tree branches. In the distance birds alarmed by the activity kept up an inquisitive chatter. But even their sharp sounds fell silent at last, and as Carlin and Hedges stood there in the autumn night the only sounds were the sharp impact of spade on stone and the deep harsh breathing of the heaving constables.

The work was arduous and tricky, for under the rubble of broken concrete and brick was a pile of loose earth. There had been no loose earth in the previous two wells. The discovery excited Carlin. He knew why someone filling in a well might use such packing.

To conceal an offensive odour.

The loose earth became mud, and the thick ooze was dredged out a spadeful at a time, and then one of the constables began coughing. The other swore.

"What's the matter?" asked Inspector Hedges, stepping forward.

"It stinks, sir, and there's water down there," one of the diggers told him.

A bucket was lowered on a rope and the well drained until the bucket was scraping up thick viscous mud again. Carlin told the men to stand back, and he picked up one of the lanterns and held it down in the mouth of the well. A heavy fetid stench rose in his face. He narrowed his eyes, twisting the the lantern in his hands until the light reached the bottom of the smelly pit.

He saw something protruding from the slimy ooze that made him hold his breath.

He thought of a woman unable to rest easy during long nights in Sydenham while she worried about her missing son. A mother who had dreamed of her son's body being at the bottom of a well.

Carlin stood back, passed the lantern to Hedges.

"Take a look," he invited.

The divisional inspector took the Yard superintendent's place and peered down the shaft of the well among the dancing shadows. He straightened abruptly.

"A body's been stuffed down there head first," he said, voice tense. "That's a foot sticking up."

"I want the men to be very careful how they remove the body," Carlin said gravely.

Extracting the body from the obnoxious ooze and raising it from the well required not only patience and time, but the exercise of considerable ingenuity. At length, however, the men hauling on the ropes slippery with stinking mud were able to get their hands on the legs. The clothed body of a young man was deposited on the pile of springy weeds at the side of the well.

Hedges came and stood beside Carlin, who said in a quiet voice, "There'll be no need to empty the other two wells, inspector."

As the men cleaned up after their gruesome and tiring task Carlin made arrangements with Hedges to have the post-mortem examination completed without delay.

A few hours later Carlin received the police surgeon's report. The body taken from the well was that of a man of Tombe's approximate age, who had been shot at close range with a sporting gun.

The shape of the crime was clear in Carlin's mind. Dyer had been broke and with no prospect of obtaining fresh funds except by robbing his partner in the stud farm. His arson plot had been a mere bluff that had been called when the insurance company refused to pay his claim on them. He had not gone to court because he knew very well his past, as well as his fire claim, would not stand close investigation.

To rob his partner meant Dyer had, first, to remove young Tombe permanently. Murder had been the only way out. A fatal accident would have been too risky. So the clergyman's son had been killed when Dyer pressed the trigger of his sporting gun, and the body had been dumped in one of the wells. All five had been filled in as a precaution.

Then Dyer had left to start drawing on his murdered partner's credit at the bank. He had been plausible, smooth, and at the same time a fool. He had made no provision for the time when the credit ran dry except to go on using bogus cheques.

So eventually he had been fettered by his own stupidity. He had realized the truth. His wartime revolver had been carried because he knew he might have to use it. He couldn't be sure that one day the middle well of the five at The Welcomes would not be cleared and its grisly secret laid bare.

When Abbott announced that he was a police officer who would like to ask Fitzsimmons some questions in the privacy of his room Dyer had jumped to the wrong conclusion.

He had thought Abbott was about to arrest him for murder.

So Ernest Dyer had kept one jump ahead of the law, but it proved to be the one really long jump that men of violence had feared for a great many years. He had decided on the quick way out. His conscience had made him a coward.

But none of this incredible drama would be told in a court of law. Indeed, the actual pattern of bold deceit and brutal conniving would never have been revealed, most likely, if a dead man's mother had not been troubled at night by a dream that to her was vividly rational and terribly true.

Carlin, before his retirement from Scotland Yard, arrested a number of notorious killers, but he tackled no case with such ironic values as that of Ernest Dyer, the killer who couldn't face arrest.

At the eventual inquest on the remains brought from the stud farm well the Reverend Gordon Tombe had to perform a public duty which won him the sympathy of all who read the story in the newspapers. He was conducted into a bare room and shown a sheeted form. The sheet was lowered from a sunken face topped with familiar curly hair. He looked at the stained clothes, the wrist-watch, the tie-pin, and the cuff links worn by the dead man.

He did not have to look at the hole in the back of the head where four lead slugs had entered to reach his son's brain.

The shocked clergyman told the coroner in a hoarse whisper that the remains he had viewed were those of his son Eric Gordon Tombe.

The young woman Carlin had interviewed earlier was called to give evidence, and she appeared with a veil over her bowed head and dressed in black. She had a story to tell that was closely integrated in the case Carlin had pieced together.

She had admitted telling Dyer she did not believe Eric Tombe had sent the telegram announcing he had been called overseas. Half in earnest, half trying to get a reaction from Dyer, she had said, "I think you've done away with him."

Dyer had gaped at her.

She had gone on, "If you don't tell me what you know, I'm going to the Yard and they can make inquiries."

Dyer found his voice. Giving her a tight grin, he had said, "We'll go together."

But she hadn't been put off by a ready show of acquiescence that could be a bluff, for she knew the kind of hard bluffing of which Dyer was capable.

"What about giving them a ring now?" she had suggested.

Dyer had gone down like a pricked balloon.

"Do that and I might as well blow my brains out," he said.

She had been shocked by the admission, and suddenly saw that, if she carried out her threat, she might become responsible for Dyer destroying himself. That was something she had no wish to live with.

When she stood down the pattern of the case was complete. There was no room for any lingering doubt. The man who had reached for a revolver in his pocket, while walking to his room in a Scarborough hotel, had known an Old Bailey jury would have no reasonable doubt as to who blew that hole in the back of Eric Gordon Tombe's head when the complete story was told.

If he hadn't tried to be too clever, by explaining his victim's absence to mutual friends, he might have stood a better chance of vanishing. But he could not vanish without funds. So it was his greed that set the snare for his own destruction.

Moreover, as her evidence at the inquest had shown, the girl was someone Dyer should have avoided. She had told the coroner she had been engaged to Tombe, and so not unnaturally an unexpected act on the part of her fiancé, and one she considered out of character, had made her suspicious of the plausible Dyer, especially as she had been made aware of a new coldness between the two men when they met one day in April 1922 in Tombe's Haymarket flat.

The coroner's jury returned a verdict of murder committed on approximately April 21st, 1922.

When Carlin walked out of the court the case that had resulted in no startling arrest, but which had made headlines and history alike, was over so far as the record was concerned. But Carlin himself felt he should at least pursue one additional line of inquiry that would have been open to him if he had still been seeking Eric Tombe's murderer.

Ernest Dyer had left a widow.

Carlin called on her.

He found her to be a woman who had been forced to live with unpleasant memories. She had for a time lived in the small cottage on The Welcomes property. After telling Carlin the little she knew about the financial arrangement between the ill-assorted partners, she mentioned what she recalled a scene that had taken place in the cottage some two months after the date Tombe had been murdered, according to the findings of the recent coroner's jury.

It was eleven at night on June 22nd. She was sitting alone and was feeling tired, and yet reluctant to go to bed for there was still some light in the sky. A sudden sound, rather like stones rattling against one of the cottage drain-pipes, startled her. She jumped up and hurried to the door. She called to her dog because the thought of some intruder scared her, and she believed her husband to be away in France on business.

The dog came bounding alongside as she opened the front door of the cottage. It sprang into the yard, barking and running up to a disused cowshed across the space in front of the cottage. At that moment someone stepped out of the shadows.

It was her husband. When she asked him in obvious surprise what he was doing there he reminded her of the state of his credit and added, "I can't afford to be seen here in daylight."

Which was hardly an answer to satisfy a lonely wife at almost midnight.

However, when Carlin left the widow he was convinced that Mrs. Dyer had heard her husband while he was engaged in the task of filling in the five wells. When she had started to walk towards him Dyer had blocked her way, saying fiercely, "Don't come over here. Get back into the house again, for God's sake!"

She had turned and walked back inside, and Dyer had made the dog follow her.

Later he had joined her, but he refused to offer anything like a satisfactory explanation. After all, how could he explain to an obviously unsettled and frightened woman that he had been occupied in losing a body?

Which, in fact, he had done quite successfully—but for a dream that haunted his victim's mother many months after both victim and murderer had died, both by violence, both by the same hand.

★ 4 ★

The Case of the Stored Corpses

Coincidence and a headache played a curious part in making possible a romantic attachment that ended not only in tragedy, but in the commission of a murder that horrified Londoners with a new grisly concept—a "trunk crime."

The headache occurred in Hastings, as did the coincidence.

That was the South Coast resort to which Beatrice Gregory and her mother went for their summer holiday in the year when the daughter had not been feeling well.

"The sea air will soon put you right, dear," the mother insisted.

It was a hot summer, and for days on end the weather was thundery. Beatrice Gregory had her headaches return. When she complained her mother said. "You must get out more, dear."

"I'm tired of the beach," the daughter confessed.

"Then try the park. The flowers are lovely, and they keep the grass so green even in this weather."

For a change, and taking her mother's advice, Beatrice Gregory went to Alexandra Park and walked past the flower-beds, absorbing their colour, pausing every now and again to study the trim beds and the effect of their bright colours against the velvet of the well-barbered greensward.

By one flower-bed she became aware of someone standing

at her shoulder. A voice said quietly, "They are lovely, aren't they?"

She looked round at the young man beside her. He was slightly taller, wore a stiff collar that seemed to be choking him, and for someone enjoying that blazing summer he appeared rather pale.

Within the space of a couple of minutes she found herself talking to him. About the flowers, the park, the people. Just chat, but she found it pleasant, and she also found herself sauntering at his side.

When she returned to her lodging her headache was gone. But next morning her mother complained of a headache.

"I've slept very badly," Mrs. Gregory told her daughter. "Go to the chemist's, dear, and get me a headache powder. My head feels as though it's about to split in two."

Beatrice Gregory left her mother and walked to the street with the row of shops that was not many minutes' from their lodging. She passed half-way down the shops before she came to a chemist's. She turned into it, and as she approached the counter a familiar face appeared on the other side.

"Why, hello," said the young man with the pale face rising from the confines of his stiff white collar. "Fancy seeing you again, and so soon. Did you know I worked here?"

"No," she admitted.

"What a coincidence," he said.

But there was no coincidence in their next meeting. The chemist's assistant, whose name was Arthur Devereux, met Beatrice Gregory each evening after finishing work. As for Beatrice, she was enchanted by such masculine company, for Devereux was a young man with a fast tongue that was also glib. He spun tales about his travels and he made everyday incidents into adventures. Perhaps it was not entirely his fault that he was able to swamp Beatrice's drab life with colour, but he did nothing to tone down the general effect.

She was captivated and enraptured.

She told her mother she was in love.

Mrs. Gregory was like a good many other Victorian mothers with a marriageable daughter, on the look-out for a likely son-in-law. She suddenly saw the chemist's assistant as a possible in this important role. She was careful to find no fault with the young man who had happened, as they said in those days, in her daughter's life.

So Mrs. Gregory stood, as it were, in the wings of the romantic drama being played in her daughter's life. She may very well have encourgaged the fulfilling of love's young dream. If she did, then the years were to bring her a terrible personal reckoning. But for the remainder of the holiday at Hastings the thundery weather was forgotten while the fair flower of romance bloomed.

Before the Gregorys returned to London the fast talker got around to the words that seemed really to matter to Mrs. Gregory. He told Beatrice he was in love with her and wanted to make her his wife.

The young couple who had met by chance in a park and within hours been thrown together again by coincidence became engaged. Mrs. Gregory settled back to take life more easily. A paramount obstacle in the life of all mothers with unattached daughters had been surmounted. Perhaps she had hoped for something better than a shop-assistant for her daughter, but she was old enough to understand that one came to terms with reality and did not set too much store by mere hopes.

However, she was due for a sharp surprise in one respect. A normal Victorian engagement running comfortably into months, perhaps even years, seemed to her in every way desirable.The man her own headache had helped to select for her son-in-law had a different conception of what was a suitable duration for an engagement.

After only a few weeks he announced that he wanted to marry Beatrice without further delay.

Mrs. Gregory felt shocked, almost affronted, by what she considered indecent modern haste. But in striving to make plain her matronly point of view she found she was in a minority. For once she found herself opposed by her daughter, and Mrs. Gregory was also reminded of the youth of the ardent young man her daughter had decided to give her heart to without much maidenly reserve. Beatrice actually was a year older than Arthur Devereux, and neither had grown out of their teens.

It may be that Mrs. Gregory had misgivings when she heard the easy and facile arguments for an early wedding. Instinctively she was against what she looked upon as a refusal to wait a respectable interval.

"You hardly know each other. You're both very young. You need to save up for a home."

Her well-intended reminders fell on deaf ears. She waged a losing contest which she could have won simply by withholding her consent as her daughter was under twenty-one. But it would have taken a braver woman than Mrs. Gregory to adopt such a course when her daughter's happiness would be placed in jeopardy. She may have had to overcome personal scruples. She may have strangled doubts as to Arthur Devereux's ability to provide for a wife and any family that came along in the almost predestined way in which families appeared to arrive for the Victorian poor.

Because on one score she had no reason for doubt at all. Mr. and Mrs. Arthur Devereux would be extremely poor. They would, in fact, begin married life condemned to back rooms in a slum property.

What such a life entailed Mrs. Gregory knew far better than the headstrong young romantics who in her presence chattered like magpies about happiness and being together and how wonderful it was being in love.

It is very doubtful whether she had ever attempted to explain what a later age called the facts of life to her daughter. Beatrice's roseate notions of romance and married bliss probably owed more to Ouida and Mrs. Henry Wood than to Mrs. Gregory.

As for Arthur Devereux, he had a spate of feelings, none of them very fine and very few of them sensitive, and he possibly knew as little of the realities of marriage and the compulsions of sex as the girl who was older than he and so obviously enjoyed his gush and flowery talk. She made him feel a man simply because she looked at him with a glance that could with reasonable truth be described as melting. It is doubtful whether he even knew he bore an exceedingly romantic name, one that had been uttered throughout England with awe in the time of the first Elizabeth.

But one could scarcely imagine two such less likely possessors of the same name as Robert Devereux, second Earl of Essex, and Arthur Devereux, unknown and under-paid chemist's assistant. Yet such is the irony of circumstance, these amazingly dissimilar Devereux males who lived three centuries apart both died at the hand of the public executioner. But then the kinship provided by death is what makes the human family one, when all blood-ties are cancelled out.

So Mrs. Gregory became a mother-in-law, and her daughter went to live in a drab little house in Kilburn with a husband who lost much of his ardour and a good many of his illusions that first week of marriage.

The wages of a chemist's assistant at the end of the nineteenth century could be better reckoned in shillings than pounds unless one enjoyed coping with the most irregular of fractions. Arthur Devereux developed a moodiness that was a bitter discovery to his wife long before his first child was born. Yet curiously it was the arrival of the delicate and weedy infant son that transported him anew to those fanciful realms where he indulged his imagination and his love for the imposing clichés of the period.

The new arrival to the Kilburn ménage was christened Stanley. To use what might be termed a fruitful metaphor, he was the apple of his father's eye, even of both eyes, for Arthur Devereux looked upon the pink speck of mortality that had thrust fatherhood upon him as a creature demanding adoration and unstinting service.

Stanley, in short, arrived to brighten his father's life and cast a long deep shadow over his mother's. There was little cash to spare to feed even so small an additional mouth, but Arthur Devereux, who had grown into the habit of belatedly counting the pence in some fond belief that the pounds would take care of themselves, begrudged his small son nothing. True, he went around telling anyone who would listen that the baby looked like him, so it could be that he saw himself assuming immortality of sorts in the person of the mewling Stanley. His son's grubby baby ways were a delight. The infant's demands provided pleasure when the father had to devote himself to fulfilling them.

It was curious, it was stupid, and it was downright unhealthy.

The wife tried to reason with her husband, only to be silenced with wellnigh brutal criticisms of herself as a mother. The mother-in-law, upon those occasions when she visited her daughter's family or was visited by them, gently chided Arthur Devereux for the way he enveloped himself in the mantle of fatherhood. She was brusquely told not to interfere.

He knew what was best for his son.

It was a sort of litany by which he lived.

His moodiness returned when he was informed his wife was again pregnant. Instead of enjoying this further flowering of his fatherhood, the chemist's assistant argued himself into seeing the coming of a new baby as the arrival of a competitor for Stanley.

That thought was like a thorn in the softest flesh of his mind.

He began to dread the arrival of the new Devereux, boy or girl. To the father who had grown an uncomfortable neurosis about his son Stanley, and about the infant's significance in his paternal parent's shoddy life, a heavy blow was about to shake his back-street world. Fate certainly played a dirtier-than-usual trick on him. At least, that was how Arthur Devereux myopically saw it.

His labouring Beatrice was in the fulness of time delivered of twins. Both were sons.

Stanley really had competition now.

The competition was offered a fair start in what was to prove a very short life by being provided with a brace of high-sounding names apiece. Lawrence Rowland and Evelyn Lancelot. Far-off days of chivalry and far-off echoes of lost romance were woven into the names that sounded oddly among the lines of freshly washed nappies criss-crossing the Kilburn back-street living room like rows of bunting at some field of tourney.

Arthur Devereux might be pocket poor, he might be moody, but when events offered him a challenge he could accept with a gay verbal flourish.

There was little else he could do to make life easier for his growing family. The weekly wage packet remained distressingly constant. But fine names could not be devoured even when one had struggled through the months before the tiny brethren were weaned.

Arthur Devereux began to despair, and despair eventually made him desperate for change. Any sort of change that would better the prospect for Stanley. But if Arthur Devereux was dangerously unbalanced in the matter of his affection for his first-born, so there was a complementary swing of the pendulum in the opposite direction to achieve some sort of even temporary equilibrium.

As his affection for Stanley was stimulated, so was his loathing of the twins with the lordly names increased. He began to see the twins as obstacles to Stanley's securing his rightful share of what the Devereux household had to offer. What they accepted as daily substance was taken from Stanley.

Money spent on clothes for them was money of which Stanley was deprived.

If he thought of himself as a provider, as someone working to earn money with which necessities and small luxuries could be purchased, then it was undoubtedly as a provider for Stanley. What the others secured was taken from Stanley.

In time, it was inevitable that arguments arose about the three children, and just as inevitably Beatrice had to champion the cause of the knightly named brethren, so that she came to be associated in the father's mind as being opposed to the interests of Stanley.

A man indulging in such unnatural fantasies was one lacking in mental stability, and this must have made itself apparent to those who employed him. The Devereux family entered a period when its resources ebbed. The provider failed, some weeks, to provide. The family lived on very short commons, and there were nights in a row when empty stomachs induced crying in the long night hours. The pattern of life became ugly. With the father finding a fresh job only to lose it because he was unable to hold it down satisfactorily, the rhythm of the Devereux household not only became uncomfortable, it came at times close to being unendurable.

Beatrice sobbed her disillusions to her mother.

Mrs. Gregory bitterly reproved herself for allowing her heart, as she thought of it, to rule her head. She gave her daughter advice on how to save her marriage from drifting to ruin. The advice arrived too late. Everything the hopeful Beatrice tried as a means of pleasing her husband and brightening the grey days of her brood served only to make him hate her.

In this sorry atmosphere Stanley achieved his sixth year, and the toddler stood erect like a miniature Arthur Devereux, which was precisely how the father saw his favourite son. He saw the twins as excess baggage on his particular pilgrimage, and he began to think of how he could shed it, and of what he could do for Stanley once he had lightened the financial load.

He might even be able to afford to send Stanley to a private school. Anyway, it should certainly be possible if there were only Stanley and himself.

Just the two of them.

Another fanciful thought grew into a fantasy. He must find a way to rid himself and Stanley of the twins and their mother. In his clouded unbalanced mind he saw the permanent disappearance of the three unwanted members of the family circle as the positive solution of all his difficulties, emotional and economic. With Stanley to himself no one could supplant him as the boy grew older. He could provide a better education, and his son would grow up grateful to his father and proud of the sacrifice made in the name of something ugly and abnormal which would be made acceptable by being called love.

The neurosis was, in point of fact, about to become an obsession.

Arthur Devereux began to scheme very much in private. There was a time when he lived as though everyday events did not concern him, and his wife again sought her mother's advice, for she was puzzled and perturbed by what she could not understand.

"You must have patience, dear," counselled the woman whose formative years had been spent in a vanishing Victorian age.

But patience merely meant suffering in silence. Beatrice Devereux was twenty-five. She looked middle-aged.

One day her husband of twenty-four came home with news.

"We're moving. I've found us a new home," he announced.

The change was done at speed. Almost within hours the family was settled in another back-street apartment. Not long afterwards the family in the rooms below told Arthur Devereux they had given notice to the landlord. He lost no time in calling on the landlord and offering extra rent to have the lower rooms remain empty. He said it was so that his family could enjoy the quiet. The landlord fixed a price which was agreed, and Arthur Devereux returned home knowing that when the people downstairs moved out he would have the house to himself and his own family.

Shortly after the Devereux family became the sole occupants of the house the father arrived home one day with a large trunk. He explained that it was to store things, but omitted to enlighten a bewildered wife as to which things were to be stored. The furnishings of the Devereux home were meagre in the extreme. It was not long after the large trunk took its place in the household that the husband decided his wife was ailing and required medicine.

"I know about physics," he said. "I'll make some up myself, so we'll save the cost."

What he made up was a lethal quantity of morphine. He induced the mother and the twins to swallow it. Stanley, apparently, was not ailing.

Before long Beatrice and the twins lay dead. He bundled the warm bodies into the large trunk, locked it, and went to bed feeling pleased with himself. After all, he now had Stanley to himself. So Stanley's future was assured.

He was wakened by a milkman who wanted to know how much milk to leave.

Devereux surprised the tradesman. "Don't bother to call any more," he told the man. "My wife and the children have gone away for a holiday. Me, I can manage."

When the milkman had left he prepared breakfast for himself and Stanley. Afterwards he tied a stout rope he had procured around the trunk and then sealed its edges. Next he took Stanley to the home of a friend, where he arranged to leave the boy while he took a journey that could not be put off. He did not explain the journey more precisely.

Actually it was to a large depository in Kensal Rise, where he asked the foreman in charge of collections to call at his home and pick up a large trunk filled with books, as well as other domestic articles.

"I shall be away some time and I want to leave them in store," he told the man."When is the earliest you can make the collection?"

"How about this afternoon?"

Arthur Devereux beamed. "That will suit me very nicely," he said.

That afternoon the large trunk, now excessively heavy, was trundled down the stairs by two hefty removal men. When the collection van had gone Arthur Devereux went out and called on a dealer with whom he soon made arrangements for disposing the few pieces of furniture Beatrice had spent hours of her young life polishing and cleaning.

Arthur Devereux was a man in a hurry to shake the dust of Kilburn from his shoes. He was also in a hurry to begin a new life. He arrived in a different neighbourhood of London, found rooms in which he installed himself and the mystified but trusting Stanley, and then set about finding a job. He certainly appeared a different person from the moody father who had worried Mrs. Gregory's daughter. He secured a job with a chemist, and then made arrangements for Stanley to attend a private school.

It was like a dream coming true. Arthur Devereux was a changed man. The trouble was he had no idea just how changed he really was; nor did he ever realize how great was that change.

The arrival of a letter from Mrs. Gregory merely caused him amusement. His mother-in-law had apparently gone to considerable pains to find his new address, and very tersely she demanded the whereabouts of her daughter. Still enjoying the curious sensation of power he felt, Devereux wrote an accommodating reply. He explained that Beatrice had found it necessary to go with the twins to the country. Their health had made the change necessary.

Mrs. Gregory was not to be put off. She replied to his letter, asking for Beatrice's present address in the country.

This request was not acknowledged, whereupon Arthur

Devereux's mother-in-law presented herself at his home and was amazed at the change she found in him. He told her he didn't wish his wife to write to her because in her present state of health writing a letter would upset her.

Mrs. Gregory stayed to argue, but argument did not produce what she had come seeking, her daughter's address. She left her son-in-law with her mind full of foreboding, and anxious to try to discover the truth of her daughter's disappearance, as she now thought of Beatrice's absence. She made inquiries in the street where the Devereux family had lodged, and someone told her of the van with the name of the Kensal Rise furniture depository written large on its side. She went to Kensal Rise, and the collection foreman passed her on to the manager, who told her of the large trunk they held for her son-in-law. When she demanded he open it he informed her that before he did that he would require authorization from a magistrate.

Mrs. Gregory took her departure and the depository manager thought he had seen the last of a busybody. He was wrong. Mrs. Gregory was on the warpath. She returned with a policeman and the order necessary for opening the trunk.

It was a very badly shaken manager who stared aghast at the stored corpses the depository had been guarding. News of the discovery reached Scotland Yard and Fleet Street about the same time. Inspector Pollard travelled to Kensal Rise, and Arthur Devereux, after reading of the opening of the large trunk, shook himself out of his new-found complacency and caught a train to Coventry.

As a fugitive he was a dismal failure. When he ran short of cash he took a job with a chemist. That was where Pollard found him.

The Yard man's appearance and his prepared questions badly rattled a young man who was beginning to get the idea that he hadn't been as smart as he had thought. He denied any knowledge of a large trunk and claimed Pollard had made a mistake, confusing him with someone else.

He was brought back to London and separated from Stanley, which made him angry. After his anger had subsided and he had listened to some advice from the Yard man who had arrested him he agreed to make a voluntary statement. It was one huge bluff.

The statement claimed:

"For months we had been very hard up. I was out of a job and food was scarce. My wife was always complaining, and she could not bear to see the twins lacking food. I think that their cries drove her mad, but at the time I had no suspicion of the fact. I went out early every morning to look for work, and it was seldom I had more than a poor breakfast and a supper of bread and cheese each day. Every penny I could raise I gave to my wife.

"One morning, just before I left, she told me that she could endure poverty no longer. 'I will kill the twins and myself,' were her exact words. 'I'd rather see them dead than starving.' I rebuked her for her evil thoughts, but of course I never imagined for a moment that she had any intention of carrying out her threat. Up to that time she had not struck me as being likely to take her own life."

He continued with his attempt to fool an astute Yard man by stretching his bluff until it was a transparent lie:

"That night I came home at half-past ten worn out, and I let myself in with my latch-key. Not a sound could I hear, but I was not surprised as I thought everybody was in bed. But the moment I entered the bedroom and saw Mrs. Devereux lying dead with the twins beside her I realized that she had carried out her threat."

He concluded with almost a flourish, as though he were close to obtaining a vicarious thrill from his precarious situation in retrospect:

"Imagine my terrible position. My wife had poisoned the twins with morphine belonging to me, and had then committed suicide by the same means. I was a chemist's assistant and in a position to get poison. No one would believe that I was not the murderer. Public opinion would convict me of the terrible crime. I lost my head and raved, but after a bit I came to the conclusion that the only thing for me to do was to hush up the whole affair. Accordingly I bought the trunk and placed the bodies in it. That's the truth, and if you don't believe it I can't help it, but I am not a murderer."

Perhaps, in the scope of his own crazy rationalizing about what was best for Stanley, he was as honest as not in considering himself to be a murderer. But he was certainly a liar, and at times a glib one. Pollard proved as much when he discovered that the trunk had arrived at the house prior to the last time Beatrice Devereux was observed by neighbours. Motive was something the legal lights could fight about. Pollard had his case, and Devereux was committed for trial at the Old Bailey.

The large trunk at the Kensal Rise depository had been opened on April 13th, 1905, an unlucky day for Arthur Devereux, who entered the dock at the Central Criminal Court to be tried before Mr. Justice Ridley in July.

Charles Elliott, who led for the defence, tried without loss of time to make capital out of the fact that there had been a good deal of hostile reporting of the case in the various national newspapers.

Mr. Justice Ridley wasn't the kind of judge to be stampeded. He informed the defence that he had no responsibility for what was said in the Press, and was very sure the chosen jury would prove themselves to be eminently impartial in their consideration of the evidence.

In short, the trial was to continue in London, where the man in the dock was currently considered to be something of an ogre. Arthur Devereux quickly decided to claim insanity. It was another of his tired and belated bluffs that did not work. The alienist called to establish whether the prisoner was sane read Devereux's own statement. He pronounced him sane within the legal definition of the term.

The trial got under way. Sir Charles Mathews, later to become a famous Director of Public Prosecutions, stripped all pretence from the flimsy defence put up. Pollard had done yeoman work in checking Devereux's movements. He had proved, for instance, that while Beatrice Devereux was alive her husband had applied for a situation that had been advertised in Hull. In his application he described himself as a widower.

He did not obtain the post.

He made a similar application elsewhere, secured a fresh post, and with his first wages bought the fatal trunk.

The jury took no great while arguing the pros and cons of the evidence put forward. They found the prisoner guilty, and Mr. Justice Ridley sentenced him to death. He was hanged at Pentonville on August 15th. When his lime-encrusted remains were interred in the prison yard a trunk crime was no longer a novelty to Londoners.

It still isn't, for Arthur Devereux has had his imitators throughout the years since he stepped down from the Old Bailey's dock, but they have been no more successful than he in losing a body that had become a hindrance and a danger.

★ 5 ★

The Case of the Black Sea-chest

Jean Videle was hanged sixty years before Arthur Devereux, and at the other side of the world, twelve thousand miles away, in Sydney. It is very doubtful if Devereux had ever heard of the Frenchman executed according to tenets of Anglo-Saxon law in another world and another age. But they both shared the same idea.

Devereux used a big tin trunk, Videle a large black sea-chest.

Apart from that their stories have nothing in common except the hempen noose into which both men fitted their necks to pay the debt society demanded of them.

Videle was a French emigrant to Australia, one of a number who around the middle of the nineteenth century made a colony along the Sydney waterfront. That waterfront had one particular section noted for its readiness to spout violence like a whale spouts salt water. It was known as Circular Quay, a self-explanatory name.

The quay lost itself in Pitt Street, while the neighbourhood took on colour where the Australian Hotel stood four-square to the winds blowing in from the harbour and the Rose of Australia public-house catered to a dockside clientèle that frequently made the night hideous with their quarrels and red-handed fights.

The inhabitants of Circular Quay might with considerable truth be described as denizens. The district was a jungle and most of the people living in it lived by the jungle rule of tooth and claw. That included some members of the French colony.

Also a certain Thomas Warne, who was a man prepared to make a living by battening on his fellows. At least, that was how his method of collecting debts for various Sydney merchants was viewed by sundry victims of his rough collecting tactics. He was a big man. He had to be to remain upright on his feet in that area. He had broad shoulders, and he needed them. He also had shoulder-length hair that covered his coat collar which he shook as a lion shakes its mane.

Not surprisingly he made few friends, but they included Jean Videle, who had been introduced to Warne by other friends, Mr. and Mrs. James Duval, also of the French colony. Along Circular Quay the new-come Frenchmen quickly had their first names anglicized, like the Duvals. Videle became John to Warne, and before long the two were boon drinking companions, and their friendship warmed to the pitch where the debt collector invited the Frenchman to take up lodgings in the three-storey house he owned in Hughes Terrace, beyond the limits of the brick and stone jungle. The rooms in the Hughes Terrace house were lit with lamps burning whale oil, and among her other duties it was the task of a servant named Ellen Todd to keep the lamps filled and their wicks trimmed. She was a girl with morals adjusted to the demands of the district in which she lived. When Videle arrived to take up lodging in the house she gave him a smile and in return he gave her an invitation to spend the nights in his room.

However, young as she was, a girl still in her teens, she was sufficiently sophisticated to realize that a too-ready acquiescence can defeat itself if it is to produce gifts and payments. So Ellen played hard to get. She shifted her mattress to the scullery when Videle came looking for her, and he became angry.

For the first time she became afraid of a man subjected to

her teasing tactics. She decided she had made a mistake in her handling of Videle, that the Frenchman was vindictive, and would probably take delight in really causing her physical harm for her egging him on.

She collected her few possessions, stuffed them into a bag, and after a sleepless night on guard against Videle's reappearance in the scullery she left the house. She did not take her leave of Warne or ask him for the wages already due to her.

She was scared and she was being sensible about it. So she thought.

When Videle found she had left in full flight he lost his temper. He told Warne he must get the girl back.

"Why?" the debt collector asked, amused at the Frenchman's display of pique and hurt pride. "You tried to get her into bed and she wasn't having it. Let her go, John. The world's full of wenches."

"I want her, Tom."

Warne laughed. "Maybe, John. But she don't want you and she's shown it. Forget her. She's gone."

Videle gave the other a shrewd look. "You've no one to clean the house now she's gone," he reminded Warne, who grinned at him.

"That's where you're wrong again, John. Oh, yes, I have someone all right."

His laugh boomed like surf breaking on a rocky shore.

"You have?"

"Sure I have." Warne laughed again, enjoying the joke and prolonging it.

"Who is she?"

"Not a she. A he, John. You!"

Warne rocked in his chair and Videle stood watching him, a twisted look on his face.

"Why me?" he asked when Warne's humour had worked itself out.

"You're a Frenchy. You can cook, you told me. Well, now's

your chance to prove it, and cleaning goes with cooking, don't it?"

Videle saw the other meant it. He said, "We'll do the work together. That fair enough?"

Warne sensed the challenge behind the words. He scowled, no longer amused. What had seemed like a damned good joke had gone sour.

"All right," he grumbled. "If that's the way you want it, John."

But Warne wasn't happy about the arrangement, and he wasn't satisfied. For one thing, he now saw the incident in a different light. Videle had lost him the services of a servant who had suited him. For another, it wasn't his habit to compromise or temporize. He remained on top in the savage world of Circular Quay because he was stronger than the next man and was able to impose his will on others. Videle had stood up to him. That was bad.

What he didn't know was that Videle, too, lived by a curious code of his own. To the Frenchman friendship was one thing, a woman was another. Warne, as he saw it, had refused to help him get the woman he wanted. To that extent Warne had denied him. To be denied was to earn Videle's enmity beyond the demands of friendship.

He cooked and cleaned the house and said nothing when Warne welshed on his share of the household chores, but he sought out a man named Turner, known to entertain a special hate for the debt collector. It was a hate cordially reciprocated by Warne. The two men had been adversaries in a court case, and by mutual lying had fouled each other's chances. Such memories slept very lightly around Circular Quay.

And with ample reason.

Turner had once tried to even the score by hiring a hard-knuckled seaman to start a quarrel with Warne in the bar of the Australian Hotel. The fight that ensued was vicious and bloody in true jungle tradition. The seaman, whose name was

Britten, not only used his fists, he clamped down with his strong yellow teeth, and one animal bite left Warne minus a little finger.

The fight ended indecisively, but a few hours later Britten was at sea. Turner decided the score was much more even and tried to intimate as much to Warne, who lifted a glass in his bandaged hand and threw the contents in Turner's face.

After that Turner's threats were so menacing that the police arrested him and in court he was bound over to keep the peace, which was a relative thing along the Sydney docks. Videle thought Turner could be an ally in paying back Warne for letting the girl get away. He knew that Turner was on good drinking terms with the Duvals, who were invariably pushed for cash to pay their debts.

It was about a month before Christmas that Videle made a move by getting the Duvals to invite him at a time when he could meet Turner. The date was November 22nd, 1844. Turner listened to what was said, and did not say much. But when he left the tavern where the meeting had taken place he was accompanied by Videle.

It was late, and even later when Warne was roused from sleep by someone banging on his door. He climbed into some clothes and went to open it.

Outside stood a couple of men. One of them, he saw as he rubbed the sleep from his eyes, was Videle.

"What's the idea coming back at this time, John?" he asked grumpily.

"Thought you'd like a drink with us, Tom."

"Hell, you got any idea of the time?"

"Never too late for a glass."

Videle laughed jerkily, playing it smooth and not being very successful, for he was showing signs of being nervous, which Warne would have noticed if he hadn't been still half asleep.

The Frenchman's companion said nothing. Warne was not able to see his face, for he stood behind Videle, and the light from behind the debt collector barely reached him.

"All right, damn it, we'll have a drink. Come on in."

Warne turned his back and started towards the wide mouth of the flame-blackened fireplace. There was a pile of kindling beside the hearth, and on top of the thin logs was an axe. The debt collector reached for the lamp to place it in a more central position. Then he turned to go for a bottle. A movement at the woodpile caught his attention, and he started to turn back.

He had time to see that the lamplight no longer struck the blade of the axe, then the shiny steel was arcing towards his head. Too late he threw up an arm and tried to jump back.

The axe-head caught him on the temple and he went down with a cry gurgling in his throat. Before he could sprawl his length on the floor the axe caught him a second time.

The debt collector's head was suddenly crimson. He made no movement.

The axe continued to rise and fall in a brutal and senseless butchery, mangling the remains, splashing the floor and walls with blood. Tom Warne had no longer any scores to be made even or debts to be collected. But his body could still take punishment even if Warne knew nothing about it.

He had been roused from his night's sleep to open his door to a pair of drunken louts lusting for blood. When the lust was slaked the killers had a fearful mess to clean up. They began by using some of the kindling to start a fire in the wide-mouthed grate. They banked up the fire until it was roaring up the chimney.

The room became as hot as an oven, for outside it was a warm, close summer night.

Warne's badly chopped body was stripped of the clothes he had donned hurriedly, and the red-smeared corpse was forced into a grotesque sitting position, with the head down between the legs, as though the dead man had to be revived from a fainting fit. The sprawled arms were pushed inward and kept in position by thrusting the grubby hands down between the naked thighs.

Tom Warne's corpse was in a trussed position.

Held in position, it was picked up by the two ruffians and carried to the blaze in the fireplace. One of them must have counted, for getting the trussed corpse on to the fire without swamping the flames and setting the place alight must have been no easy piece of manipulating, especially in the oven-like temperature of the room.

But they managed. With fearful dexterity they worked that grisly joint for roasting on to the fire in the broad hearth and balanced it among the flames so that Tom Warne with his hands and head between his legs sat there among them like some outlandish salamander, his blood sizzling, his pale body charring and turning black, his hair spinning from his skull in fiery wisps.

And of course the cooking corpse stank. Richly and obscenely.

The stench filled the room so that Videle felt his stomach suddenly starting in a panic towards his throat. For there was plenty of tallow on Warne's bones. Some of it flared like a pine-knot, hissing at the clustered soot smeared around the chimney's gaping mouth, and set it alight. Festoons of ignited soot that stank with an acrid, sulphurous stench drifted low in a sudden down draught and floated into the room to start miniature fires.

A different kind of panic sent Videle's stomach hurrying back to where it more or less belonged. He gagged on the sharp odour of burning soot.

"We'll have the damned place alight if we don't do something quick," he shouted. "Can't you see—the chimney's on fire!"

His companion decided the only way to tackle the conflagration Tom Warne had become was for Videle himself to scramble up on the roof and toss buckets of water down the roaring chimney.

"You are more nimble than me," he insisted. "I'll pass up the buckets to you. We've plenty of water in the butt."

Which was true, as Videle saw when he turned to look at the water-butt in the corner, at which the other man pointed. The butt was three parts full.

As Videle hesitated the other man turned on him with a show of anger.

"Go on, for God's sake. You said something's got to be done. Do it."

Grumbling, wiping sweat from his face, the Frenchman opened a window and clambered up to the roof. A bucket that slopped almost as much water as it continued to hold was passed to him. Hugging it to his chest he began to crawl along the roof towards the chimney belching smoke and sparks. He reached it, straightened, and pitched the bucket's contents down among the black and red pennants of smoke.

Steam spurted back in his face before he could duck down out of the way.

Cursing, he crawled back for more water.

It was an idiotic performance by a sodden drunkard. Videle made his monkey-like performance with the slopping bucket several times before the chimney showed signs of the fire being quenched. If he had remained in the room with the water-butt and simply doused the fireplace, presumably he could have achieved the same result with much less effort and in much less time than it took clambering about the roof in the dark.

In any case, the roof-top performance was one that demanded an audience. Not surprisingly one was provided in the person of Harriet Hodgkinson. She was an unlovely creature who graced Circular Quay with quarrelsome ways and a strident voice full of harsh Cockney vowels.

The drifting soot and the stench brought Harriet from her

room to yell imprecations into the night. Getting no satisfaction from her blasphemous protests, she started into the street to explore, and looking up saw the curious sight of a man in his shirt-sleeves pouring water down a chimney.

"What the hell do you think you're doing?" she yelled.

It was Harriet's shouted demands that awakened other neighbours and brought heads to peer from opened windows. Videle stood on the roof, suddenly scared like an actor who had forgotten his lines, and waved his arms at the only partially visible audience that was shouting its imprecations at him.

The Frenchman who had some while before almost lost his stomach now certainly lost his head.

He yelled back imprecations of his own. It was a way of relieving his tensed-up feelings and reassuring himself. But it was far from being the best way because he forgot, in his excitement, to yell in his normal accent. Instead his voice became very French.

Later no one could recall having seen clearly the face of the the man on the roof who flourished his arms and wielded a bucket, but quite a few local inhabitants remembered the voice.

Harriet's yelling also attracted the attention of a man whose job was to be attracted by such incidents. When he heard her yelling he started to find out the cause. He was a constable named Peter Thompson, and before he reached Harriet he saw the sparks filtering up to the sky and smelled the stench of burning soot mixed with another warm stench he could not place.

However, by the time he arrived at the house where Videle had put on his midnight matinée windows were being slammed shut again, and even Harriet Hodgkinson had disappeared inside her front door. The sparks had vanished among the stars, the stench remained, but there was no sign of a man on a roof, and Constable Thompson cleared his throat, spat, and passed on.

If he had been a few minutes earlier he might have walked into a real-life nightmare.

However, Constable Thompson was later to remember the time he started to return to his normal waterfront patrol, and that was to prove important in a trial that was one of the most exciting court-room dramas held in Sydney in the middle of the nineteenth century.

While the constable was walking back to Circular Quay Videle was drying himself in the room where a minor holocaust had been drenched. Filthy water trickled across the floor, littered with charred and still smoking pieces of wood. The fire in the hearth was out, but resting on the remains of the quenched blaze was the partly roasted corpse of the late Thomas Warne, continuing to exude an offensive odour of scorched flesh, burned hair, and parboiled tallow.

The two ruffians now hauled back into the room the horrendous relic of their mutual rage and spleen. By this time their stomachs must have settled themselves to accepting the ghastly demands made on their stability, for what the pair now proceeded to do they performed without puking and without going out of their minds.

Grabbing the streaming, stinking mass that was their half-cooked victim, they staggered with it back into the room and dumped it on the wet floor.

"What the hell can we do with him now?" asked Videle's companion.

"We must cut him up," the Frenchman decided.

"How can we do that?"

"There's a saw around somewhere. I've seen it," said the man who had lived in the house.

So Videle went in search of the saw he remembered, and after some minutes he came back brandishing it.

"I found it. I told you," he said as though he had done something to crow about. "Now we can cut him in half and half of him we can handle."

The grim logic of this was accepted in silence by the man who had been talked into this terrible escapade over several glasses of rotgut whisky.

But he had a question that was quite pertinent.

"What do we do with him when he's cut in half?" he inquired.

Videle stopped brandishing the saw in the light of the lamp and waved his other hand.

"There is a sea-chest somewhere. I remember it is black. We will put him in that."

He seemed happy about the idea, so his companion raised no further questions. He moved to join Videle, and between them they began the grim business of separating the charred legs from the blistered and burned torso. When Videle threw down the saw its teeth were blunted and his arm ached. He muttered in French. Although his companion did not know what the words meant he had the impression that Videle was still angry at Tom Warne. Probably because, with the marrow dried out of his bones, they were hardened and resistant to knurled and toothed steel. Well, murderers had to learn to take the rough with the smooth.

History was not to treat Jean Videle as any exception to a harsh rule.

The Frenchman went searching for the black sea-chest, and when he found it started to drag it to the room that had been turned into a filthy abattoir. The chest was opened, and the two men lifted the legless torso,with the head still tucked lower than the shoulders, and squeezed it between the sides of the chest. The severed legs were then doubled up and added to the end of the torso, so that the whole grisly contents of the chest looked like a complete body with limbs and joints.

Videle's companion was about to swing down the heavy lid of the sea-chest when he was stopped by a cry from the Frenchman.

"Wait a minute. There's something else."

Videle crossed the room and produced a grimy bag that had belonged to Warne. He did not open it, and he did not explain why the disreputable old bag had to join the remains of its owner. He threw it on top of Warne's bowed head and said, "Now."

The lid slammed down. A padlock secured it.

An hour later Videle was alone with the locked sea-chest. He was tired, and he stared at a bottle he and his companion in murder and mutilation had emptied. He turned his gaze to the sea-chest, and suddenly felt very sober.

Jean Videle looked out of the window through which he had crawled on to the roof and back again. Before long it would be daylight.He knew he had to hurry, and now he was on his own, which was perhaps as well.

He brought Ellen Todd's cleaning mop from its corner, filled the bucket from the water-butt, and set about cleaning up the mess. Just possibly he may have reflected that he was doing what Tom Warne had told him he should, and that Warne was again not helping.

There was light in the sky by the time he had finished. He started a fresh fire in the grate, and fried four eggs over the flames. The eggshells were left on the hearth. No longer hungry he lay down on the floor he had mopped and went to sleep. Beside him was the black sea-chest.

Jean Videle was not a man troubled by sensitivity.

Hours later he stopped a seafaring man about to leave the Black Dog Tavern and asked him if he wanted to earn some easy money. Tom Wilson had empty pockets, but a few scruples. He asked what he would have to do for the money.

"Carry a sea-chest to the quay," he was told.

Tom Wilson was a big man, but he staggered when he got his arms around the black sea-chest and lifted it.

"Can't carry this myself. It would break my back," he complained. "But I can lift one end."

However, it required both Jean Videle and James Duval

to match his strength and lift the other end. Between them the three men staggered with the sea-chest from Hughes Terrace to Waterman's Wharf, where a sleeping boatman was roused and offered two shillings to row the sea-chest across to some point on the North Shore.

"I'll pay when we get there," said Videle.

The boatman agreed, and started to help the others lift the weighty black chest into the moored boat. On the point of easing the chest over the edge of the wharf, the boatman suddenly pulled back, and the chest was dumped on the stone slabs above the boat.

"What have you got inside?" the boatman demanded. "It smells horrible."

"Pork," Videle told him.

"Well, I'm not taking it to North Shore," the boatman decided aggressively. "It must be rotten. Get it off the wharf."

A scuffle began, Videle trying to drag the sea-chest over the edge of the wharf, the boatman, whose name was King, trying just as hard to haul the chest away from his boat. Videle and King began swearing and shouting at each other, and before many minutes, with the strange tug-of-war still undecided, a small crowd had collected which offered ribald advice in loud voices, and the general clamour attracted the attention of a constable, who demanded to know what the fuss was about. The bemused man could make little of the references to pork and North Shore, but the stench from the sea-chest had made itself manifest, and he collared Duval and Videle and started back with them to Hughes Terrace, ostensibly to get the key that would unlock the sea-chest.

As soon as the three had gone the crowd dragged the black chest to the light outside the Waterman's Arms, and one of the more curious began prising up the lid. When it fell back they were suddenly silent.

A short while later Videle was in custody at the Harrington Street watch-house. The jailer saw him try to throw something away. It was a ring that had belonged to Tom Warne. When challenged the Frenchman, excited and almost unintelligible, claimed the ring was his because he had given Warne a whale's tooth for it.

"And a pigeon," he added when he saw the looks of disbelief on his listeners' faces.

The inquest was held two days later in the Sydney police headquarters building, which was known oddly as the Post Office, where Videle found he had three fellow-prisoners, Turner, Wilson, and Duval. When the hearing was ended Videle was kept in custody with Duval. Wilson and Turner were freed. The authorities took evidence from Harriet Hodgkinson and her neighbours and from Constable Thompson and customers who had been at the tavern where Videle had been drinking with Duval and Turner. It was impossible to decide who had accompanied Videle to the house where Warne was murdered, but there could be no doubt about the Frenchman. Harriet had recognized his voice. It was the voice of the man on the roof the night of the murder.

So Videle was charged with murder and lodged in the old Woolloomooloo Jail. Just after Christmas his brief trial passed into history and he was sentenced to be hanged, for the law had conveniently assumed as he was the only one actually known to be in the house he must, therefore, have wielded the murder weapon.

He stoutly maintained his innocence.

When he realised he could not alter the course of the inevitable he refused to co-operate in any social function, and became a nuisance to his jailers, who longed for the arrival of the February morning that would release them from the responsibility of coping with a human animal.

When that morning dawned Videle had to be forcibly cleaned and dressed before being dragged to a gallows before which stood a crowd of four thousand. The shouting and catcalls died when a priest approached the doomed man. He appeared to hold a whispered conversation with the prisoner before stepping aside and allowing the hangman to make the necessary adjustments to his gear and the Frenchman's fetters.

The shouting was commencing again when the priest held up his hand and in fresh silence announced, "The prisoner has confessed and made his peace with his Maker."

The crowd stared at Jean Videle, who stared back at the sea of faces as the hangman stood with his noose poised over the prisoner's bared head.

Videle called to the crowd.

"Pray for me—please pray for me!" he shouted.

The noose fell over his head, tightened around his neck. A few in the crowd fell on their knees. Others followed. It was as though the vast crowd was under a spell of mass hypnotism. When the hangman pulled the bolt of the trap-door under Jean Videle's tied feet no one was left standing in the square before the prison gate.

The hanging of Tom Warne's murderer became a legend in the Sydney of future ages.

★ 6 ★

The Case of the Missing Fingertips

A COUPLE of miles north of Moffat, on the Carlisle-Edinburgh road a bridge crosses a stream which is a small tributary of the River Annan. When Susan Johnson stopped on the bridge to look down at the gurgling stream she saw what appeared to be a parcel at the water's edge. The stream ran through a steep ravine, and as she continued across the bridge she glanced back and down again, and this time she received a shock.

Something was protruding from the parcel, and she was very sure it was a human arm.

Her walk that September day in 1935 was interrupted by the sight. She hastened back to the hotel where she was staying with her brother. Alfred Johnson was a man of action who could come to a quick decision. When his sister told him what she had seen he started off for the bridge, peered over, and decided she hadn't been suffering from an hallucination. He climbed from the bridge down into the ravine and bent over the soggy paper-wrapped bundle. Under the paper was some stained sheeting, which held parts of a human body. He climbed back from the ravine, aware that he had stepped straight into the middle of a mystery drama that would make headlines from Land's End to John o' Groats.

In actual fact the headlines made by the mystery extended clear across the world.

Sergeant Sloan went down into the ravine after Alfred Johnson had reported his find to the Moffat police, and he recovered three more bundles containing human remains. Two of the bundles contained heads. The flesh in each bundle was in an advanced state of decomposition and crawled with writhing yellow maggots.

When the chief constable of Dumfriesshire invited Professor John Glaister of Glasgow University and Dr. Gilbert Millar of Edinburgh University to examine the human remains it was supposed that they were parts of both male and female bodies. The four bundles were dispatched to the department of anatomy at Edinburgh University, and Professor James Couper Brash began the task of putting together the most obnoxious jigsaw puzzle he had ever encountered. He had to place the relevant portions of rotten flesh in position to make relevant bodies. The task was so formidable that he was helped by Professor Sydney Smith and Dr. Arthur Hutchinson, both of Edinburgh University's faculty of medicine.

It was when this team had been at work for some time the discovery was made that there were no portions of male anatomy in the various bundles. All the remains were female.

However, the mystery was made even more obscure by the further discovery that the total sum of the parts found did not comprise two complete bodies.

When this disturbing fact was reported to the police a search was made along the River Arran and the stream that was its small tributary, the Linn. The almost profligate dispenser of human parts was found to have discarded other portions of female anatomy along the potamic route he or she had chosen. The searching police recovered some large pieces of decomposed flesh, a pelvis, and a water-wasted left thigh. A month after Susan Johnson had glanced back and made out the form of a human arm in the ravine the search was still continuing. It was on October 28th, at a place called Johnson Bridge, which was some nine miles from Moffat, a bundle wrapped in a newspaper was recovered. It contained a left foot. The newspaper wrapping was a copy of the *Daily Herald* with the dateline August 31st.

A week later, on November 4th, another newspaper bundle was found in a weed-strewn ravine leading away from the main Edinburgh road. It contained a right hand and forearm, and apparently the person responsible for disposing of the remains was a constant reader of the *Daily Herald*, for the dateline on this copy was September 2nd.

When all these finds had been reported the police noticed one peculiarity. All had been made on the left-hand side of the road. It was reasonable to suppose that someone travelling in a car had tossed the various bundles away while *en route* to Edinburgh. The police were sure they had a murder case on their hands, indeed a multiple murder case, for it was equally reasonable to suppose that the bodies had been dismembered and cut up because they were the remains of victims who had been killed violently. A good deal of local information about weather and rainstorms was provided, and it was fixed, as a working hypothesis, that the last day for discarding the remains that had been recovered would have been September 19th.

The reasoning that went to this was simple but with a factual basis in those local conditions. For one thing, the various bundles had been found above the level of the stream and the river. It was established that during the night of September 18th and during the morning of the next day an exceptionally heavy rainstorm had swollen the local streams to a higher-than-normal level. Assuming the bundles had actually been thrown into the swift-running floodwaters, then they had been deposited where found by the streams when their levels were going down as the floodwaters subsided.

But the extensive inquiries conducted at this stage produced no one who remembered seeing a car pull up on a bridge or along any stretch of that A 701 road which skirts the Devil's .

Beef Tub and crosses the Tweedsmuir Hills. Lists of missing persons were checked. None appeared to have been reported from the region of Dumfries or Peebles. That left the police with what seemed like a single clue.

The various wrappings used to enfold the grisly hunks of human flesh included articles of clothing, among which were a child's woolly rompers and bedlinen, and a copy of the *Sunday Graphic*, with a dateline September 15th.

A close examination of the Sunday newspaper revealed that it was a copy of what was technically known as a "slip edition." That is an edition of a limited number run off for distribution in a particular area and carrying certain local items of interest in that area. This particular "slip edition" of the *Sunday Graphic* had been for the area of Lancaster and Morecambe. It was limited to 3700 copies, and its special front-page make-up held pictures of incidents and persons at Morecambe Carnival. The local news also appealed to readers in that area.

The Dumfries police, informed of this, began a fresh search into lists of missing persons reported around mid-September and details about them. It was during this news coverage that an item in the Glasgow *Daily Record* was turned up which reported the disappearance of a young woman named Mary Rogerson. She had been working for the family of a Parsee doctor who had a practice in Lancaster.

Apparently the doctor, whose name was Ruxton, had on October 10th, just eighteen days before Susan Johnson looked over the little bridge spanning the Gardenholme Linn, to give the Annan tributary its full name, reported to the police that his wife and their maid had been missing since September 15th.

The chief constable of Dumfries received a report from the Lancaster police. It was more than merely interesting. For instance, Dr. Ruxton had gone to the police with a dual complaint. He not only wanted his wife and their maid found, but he was annoyed by what he described as loose talk in the district. He claimed it was ruining his practice as a medical man.

That, too, was very relative, for Dr. Ruxton had reputedly the largest medical practice in Lancaster.

More information about the Parsee doctor was sought and provided by the Lancaster police. He had arrived in the town five years before, in 1930, and his medical degrees included those of bachelor of medicine and bachelor of surgery. He was a native of Bombay whose original name was rather a mouthful.

Bukhtyar Rustomji Ratanji Hakim.

Not very surprisingly when he arrived in England to set up a medical practice he shortened it to the more easily remembered Buck Ruxton. He was married to an Englishwoman, and was the father of three children. The Ruxtons, up to the time of the disappearances, had lived at 2 Dalton Square, Lancaster.

The Dumfries police also learned that the information gleaned by the *Daily Record's* reporter about Mary Rogerson the maid had been supplied by the missing girl's stepmother.

While the forensic experts in Edinburgh were still engaged in examining minutely the various pieces of human remains that had been recovered from the river-banks some of the clothing used for wrapping was photographed.

The national newspapers were supplied with copies of the photos of the woolly rompers and of a woman's blouse that had been cleaned. The blouse had a patch under one arm. When Mary Rogerson's stepmother saw the picture and read about the patch she went to the police.

"That's one of my blouses," she said. "I gave it to Mary after I'd put that patch under the arm."

So suddenly the investigation had not only direction, but also a very useful starting point.

Mary Rogerson's stepmother had other information for the police. She told them of a Mrs. Holme, who lived in Grange-over-Sands. She had given the stepdaughter some clothes for the Ruxton children, whom she had come to know when the family stayed with her for a holiday in the previous June. Mrs. Holme was in due course shown the woolly rompers.

She too recognized her own handiwork.

"This is a pair I gave Mary," she assured the police.

"How can you be so sure?" she was asked.

"By this knot. I distinctly recall tying it."

She worked loose the elastic in the woolly suit and showed that a knot had been tied in it to take up some slack.

"That's the knot I tied," she insisted.

This positive identification was set beside other evidence obtained by detectives investigating events in Dalton Square on and immediately after September 15th.

It was on the 15th, they learned, that Ruxton had called at the home of Mrs. Oxley, who came daily to clean the Parsee's home.

"I thought I'd tell you, Mrs. Oxley," he told her, "there's no need for you to come today."

Mrs. Oxley was surprised at this show of consideration from a man who had always appeared to take both her and her work very much for granted.

Inquiry produced the information that on the same day Ruxton had called at a garage and bought two gallons of petrol in a can. He gave a bloodstained suit and some stained carpet to a panel patient, Mrs. Hampshire, in the afternoon. He had called on her at four o'clock and asked her if she could give him a hand getting ready for the decorators who were coming. He added that his wife and Mary Rogerson were away on holiday.

"Mrs. Ruxton is in Blackpool," he explained.

But at eleven o'clock that morning he had told Mrs. White-side that he was unable to attend to her small son as he was getting ready for the coming decorators and his wife was in Scotland.

An hour later, almost on the stroke of noon, he had arrived

at the home of a dental surgeon named Anderson who lived in Morecambe and requested Mrs. Anderson to look after his children until the next day. He was alone with them, he said, because his wife had gone with the maid on holiday. He did not say where, but he flourished a bandaged hand. He claimed he had cut it while opening a tin of peaches for the children that morning.

Tom Partridge, who had a newspaper round, told the police he had delivered the *Sunday Graphic* that morning at 2 Dalton Square. He had pushed the paper under the door because he had received no reply to his knocking. Ruxton, however, had already bought the *Sunday Graphic* from a newsagent on his way back from Mrs. Oxley's. Something else that was unusual and probably significant was Ruxton's refusal at ten o'clock to allow Mrs. Hindson, who had come with two quarts of milk, the regular order, to carry the bottles through to the kitchen, as she normally did.

"Just leave them on the hall table," he instructed her.

It was the first time he had personally opened the door to her, and she was surprised. Perhaps she showed it, and that may have been why he told her his wife had taken the children on holiday.

Whatever he had been engaged on that Sunday, the Parsee doctor had been a worried man. He had been furtive and secretive and behaving like a man labouring under some inner compulsion. If he had a guilty secret he had behaved like a fool by drawing attention to his acts and causing various people to remember them.

For instance, the garage where he procured the petrol was one at which he did not normally call. But he was remembered because he was dark-skinned. As though that was not sufficient, he asked for petrol in a can that had no screw stopper, and the attendant on the pumps had to hunt around to find a cork that would fit.

In the quiet of the September evening he must have realized

how foolish some of his acts had been. The next morning he tried to rectify one by arriving at the home of Mrs. Hampshire, opening the door and walking straight in without knocking, and asking in a choked voice as soon as he saw her, "Where's the suit?"

She thought he looked ill. He hadn't shaved, and under his old and dirty raincoat he was not wearing a collar or tie. He looked more like a labourer than a professional man.

The suit was folded up and lying on the table. The woman pointed to it, whereupon he seized it and said he hadn't understood that it was so stained.

"I must have it cleaned before I give it to you," he said, his knuckles pale through his dark skin as he clutched the suit tightly, as though glad to have regained possession of it.

"Oh, you don't have to bother, doctor," Mrs. Hampshire told him. "I'm glad to have the suit. We'll pay for having it cleaned."

He shook his head as though to clear it, thrust the suit at her and said, "Look in the pocket," pointing to the inside breast pocket. Inside it she found the tailor's label bearing Ruxton's name.

"Lend me your scissors," he said.

But because his right hand still wore a bandage he found he could not cut with the scissors she passed him, so Mrs. Hampshire took them from him, snipped out the label, and he waved a hand at her.

"Burn it. Now," he said insistently.

She threw the tailor's label on the fire, and he stood watching it burn, a half-smile on his face.

The woman was very concerned at this strange behaviour on the part of a man she had hitherto considered someone she could appeal to when she was sick. But now obviously he was himself sick.

She somewhat hesitantly suggested he should go home and

send for his wife. She added that she thought Mrs. Ruxton should be informed that he was ill.

"I don't want to bring her back from her holiday," he said.

It would have been more truthful if he had admitted that he couldn't. By that time Isabella Ruxton was dead and her dismembered and parcelled body ready for scattering about the Scottish countryside.

While the police were piecing together events relating to Buck Ruxton's curious behaviour in Lancaster the forensic experts in Scotland were performing a few miracles of science.

Two incomplete female bodies had been established from the recovered decomposed parts. The first had arms and forearms and hands without fingers, thighs, legs, a foot, a torso and a head. The second had arms and forearms with hands, thighs, legs, and feet, no torso but a head.

Identity was a crucial challenge.

The first body was that of a woman who had been between thirty-five and forty-five years old, height about five foot three, with high forehead and cheekbones, long jawbones, pendulous breasts, and a curious uneven bridge to her nose. She had most likely borne several children.

An attempt had been made to remove all hair by sawing away the scalp, but a few hairs remained and were of a medium brown shade. Eyes, ears, nose, lips, and facial skin had all been removed to make identification impossible, and the finger ends had similarly been removed to make sure the woman's fingerprints could not been secured. Teeth had been extracted.

Someone had done a thorough and a terribly gruesome job.

The second body was of a younger woman, probably around twenty, and quite short in stature, only four feet ten inches. There were vaccination marks on the right arm and some remaining hair was of a lighter shade than the older woman's. The right thumb had been skinned, obviously to remove a tell-tale scar that might make identification easy, but the condition of the fingernails pointed to someone who had performed heavy housework or manual labour of some kind. Other pieces of skin had been removed from various parts of the body, but in this case it was possible to take fingerprints.

Whoever had engaged in dissecting and dismembering the bodies had surgical skill and know-how.

Professor Glaister pointed out another feature that was extremely significant. There was almost a total absence of congealed blood in both bodies, and this could be explained by the severing of the arteries during the actual task of cutting up the two women. Only a practised surgeon could have done this successfully.

By the time the police were handed the results of this brilliant laboratory work, with enough positive points to help them identify the pieced-together remains, they had uncovered more facts about Ruxton's behaviour after leaving Mrs. Hampshire's house on the Monday morning.

On that Monday morning Mrs. Oxley found the hall light burning when she arrived. She had to wait until Ruxton returned from Mrs. Hampshire's before she could enter the house to begin her normal cleaning work. Then she was surprised to find that the doctor's own room, the lounge and the dining-room, all on the first floor, were locked and the keys removed. Normally the keys remained in the locks. In the garden was a mound of ash and burned refuse that had not been there when she left on Saturday.

Later Mrs. Hampshire came and did some work about the house. It was as though he felt he could trust her. He told her the regular charwoman was sick. She told him quite frankly that there didn't appear to be anything to do.

"I don't know why you asked me to come, doctor," she told him.

"You give me courage," he said, smiling.

A strange reply.

"You could send for Mrs. Ruxton," she pointed out.

He shook his head. "She's in London," he said.

By this time Mrs. Hampshire was more than curious. She did not enjoy being the recipient of lies, and said so quite bluntly. This evoked a display of apparent honesty, which was another lie, only she could not be sure.

"My wife has left me and gone off with another man, Mrs. Hampshire. I am the most unhappy man in the world."

Well, there had been talk about Mrs. Ruxton having been first married to a Dutchman and living with the doctor in London before securing a divorce. This rumour was in the main correct. What was also true, but unknown to Mrs. Hampshire and most people in Lancaster who knew the Ruxtons, was that after obtaining her divorce Isabella Van Ess *née* Kerr had not bothered to marry her Parsee doctor lover.

That evening Ruxton told a man named Edmondson that his wife and the children were in Scotland on holiday. His stories were beginning to catch up on themselves.

Thursday, September 19th, was apparently notable for two interesting features, as the inquiring detectives learned.

Mrs. Oxley arrived at her usual early hour and found Ruxton bustling around getting ready to visit a specialist about his injured right hand, as he claimed. He asked her to cook him some breakfast. Afterwards he brought the car to the back gate, closed the door of the kitchen, where Mrs. Oxley was washing up, and then made several trips to the car carrying some bulky parcels wrapped in newspaper.

Half an hour after noon he drove carelessly through the streets of Kendal, and knocked a cyclist named Beattie from his machine, which was badly damaged. The cyclist reported the accident and gave the number of a car which had not stopped. Ruxton was stopped by a crossroads traffic constable after the car's number had been circulated. Beside him on the front seat was his youngest child. When asked if he had been involved in an accident with a cyclist he said he might have. He was on his way to Lancaster after driving to Carlisle. As he did not have his car insurance certificate or driving licence in his pocket he was told to take them to the police station in Lancaster.

When he arrived with them he told a tale of having lost his way and returning by Windermere and Kendal. He said the report of having wrecked Beattie's cycle was fantastic. He had been in a hurry to get back in time for his regular surgery.

Mrs. Hampshire was one of the panel patients who attended that surgery on the 19th. No sooner had she come through the door than he rose and said quickly, "Did you send that suit of mine to the cleaner's?"

His abruptness alarmed her.

"Oh, yes, doctor," she said. Which was not the truth. The suit worried her. It had since she had tried to clean the stained stair carpet he had given her at the same time as the suit. She had used a broom and thirty buckets of water on the carpet, and when she had stopped scrubbing it because her arms were tired the water running off the carpet was still tinged a faint pink.

There were odd pieces the police fitted into their chain of evidence, too. Such as Ruxton's comment to Mrs. Oxley that made the woman give him an old-fashioned look.

"Suppose I'm driving along," he said, "and I run over a rabbit and get blood on my tyres. Won't people think I've committed a murder?"

Mrs. Oxley was also the person he tried to impress about that first report of the Moffat remains being those of a man and a woman. He held up a copy of the day's *Daily Express* and said, "You see, a man and a woman, Mrs. Oxley. Not our two."

The charwoman was well and truly mystified by this time.

"Where is Mrs. Ruxton?" she asked.

He folded the newspaper and said in an offhand manner, "She's in Lincoln Square, Birmingham."

Mrs. Curwen was another woman who occasionally worked in the Ruxton house. She found in the yard the remains of a large bonfire. Curious, she poked over the ashes and charred debris, and found several pieces of female clothing. One was part of a coat with a distinctive pattern. She had seen Mary Rogerson wearing that coat.

The man who was living with tormenting memories became fanciful on the 20th. He asked Bessie Philbrook, when he called on her, if she had been aware Mary Rogerson was pregnant. When she proved astounded by the suggestion he hinted that his wife had taken the girl away to arrange for an abortion.

By September 22nd patients were refusing to let him minister to their ailments. They were disturbed by his apparent vagaries and the obviously disturbed state of his mind.

So for a week after the 15th the rumours started to circulate, and Ruxton tried his boldest bluff. He went to the police and complained of the harm they were doing his practice. He asked the officer he saw to issue a statement to the Press disclaiming any connection between the finding of the bodies near Moffat and the absence of the two women of his own household. He was given a very soft answer. When the police were assured that was indeed the case they would be pleased to give such a statement to the Press. They were just completing their investigation.

It was soft enough, anyway, to turn away Ruxton's wrath. His anger at the rumours subsided, and the police began checking the Ruxton family's movements prior to the 15th. It had been established that the couple who called themselves Mr. and Mrs. Ruxton had frequently indulged in noisy scenes and quarrels which terminated in extravagant reconciliations which the woman enjoyed. But there was reason for believing Ruxton was jealous of the attentions he thought Isabella Ruxton was receiving from a young man employed in the office of the local town clerk. Mrs. Ruxton drove with the young man's family to visit her sister in Scotland, but circumstances conspired to make her spend the night in the same hotel as the family who had invited her to travel with them. That was on September 7th.

The next morning Ruxton arrived at the hotel in a furious temper and accused his wife of sleeping with the young man. It was an utterly false accusation, for they had occupied separate rooms.

Seven days later, on the 14th, Mrs. Ruxton went by herself to meet her sisters in Blackpool. They had gone to see the seasonal illuminations. She had done this regularly since coming north. She left Blackpool to return to Lancaster just before midnight.

None of her friends or relatives saw her again. But on the morning of the 15th the Ruxton car, a Hillman Minx, was back in the garage at 2 Dalton Square.

Police officers called at the Ruxton home. They found many fingerprints that matched those of the younger of the two dead women and they gave the second body a name. Mary Rogerson. It was now certain that Dr. Buck Ruxton had cut up the bodies of his dead wife and their servant. But was he a murderer?

He was asked to make a statement and wrote a few pages which he headed "My Movements." They were vague in the extreme and seemed slanted to prove an alibi based on the fact that Mary Rogerson was alive on the 14th. He was asked for a fresh statement, which the police took down. He took over an hour to read it through after it had been typed. He made a number of alterations.

The next morning he was charged with Mary Rogerson's murder. He seemed amazed, as well he might be. He had cut off one set of fingertips and either forgotten the others or thought they were not important.

It was what might be termed the mistake of his life. It was certainly a mistake that contributed significantly to his death at the hands of the public hangman in Strangeways Prison on May 12th, 1936.

By that time a memorable trial had passed into the history of the British criminal courts, and it is ironic that he was actually tried for the murder of Isabella Buxton "on a day between the 14th and 15th days of September, 1935, at Lancaster."

A great deal of medical evidence was forthcoming at that trial, much of it highly technical and difficult for the layman to appreciate in full, but X-ray skull photographs super-imposed on a studio portrait photograph of Isabella Ruxton proved that her face in life had fitted the skull of the older woman's body.

Dr. Shannon, the medical officer of Strangeways, gave evidence that the cut on Ruxton's right hand could not have been made with a tin-opener, but much more likely with a surgeon's scalpel. It was established that a sheet on Mrs. Ruxton's bed had an identical weaving fault to that found in the sheet recovered from the Dumfriesshire ravine. A textile expert said the two sheets had been woven on the same loom.

Giving evidence in his own behalf the prisoner said of his life with Isabella Ruxton, "We were people who could not live with each other and could not live without each other." He added as though speaking the words to himself, "Who loves most chastises most." Dr. Ruxton himself was the only witness for the defence.

When the jury retired they had a gruesome picture in their minds of the Parsee doctor meeting his wife as she came in and attacking her on the stairs, to judge by the blood that had soaked into the carpet. Most likely Mary Rogerson came to the aid of her mistress and suffered a similar fate. Then began the horrible dismemberment and removing of identification marks in the bathroom.

The jury were little more than an hour considering their verdict. When they filed back into the court-room at the Manchester Assizes their verdict was another demonstration that the murderer who successfully loses a body is indeed the exception. That description could not be applied to Dr. Buck Ruxton.

★ 7 ★

The Case of the Church Nudes

Mr. and Mrs. E. G. Noble of San Francisco were a respectable middle-class couple who regularly attended divine service at the Emmanuel Baptist Church in Bartlett Street. Early in the spring of 1895 they had two nieces from Montana staying with them, and naturally the girls went to church with their uncle and aunt.

The girls were Blanche and Maud Lamont, whose home was in Dillon, and they were on a protracted visit south to help Blanche recover from a period of ill-health that had puzzled doctors and worried her parents. Maud had gone along to keep her sister company.

The teen-age sisters liked California and Blanche soon became one of the Reverend Mr. Gibbon's church helpers in Bartlett Street, and a familiar figure in the schoolroom of the large Baptist church. The church building had been designed to support a tall roomy steeple and it had been provided with a schoolroom and library that were very much the pastor's pride and quite frequently his joy. But although Mr. Gibbon's congregation was devoted to his interest and that of his church, it is a fact that the Emmanuel Baptist Church did not enjoy an altogether salutary reputation.

It had been built in the early seventies, and the varnish on its door was scarcely dry when during a violent thunderstorm it was struck by lightning and the structure badly damaged. It was repaired at some cost to the private pockets of its trustees, but its funds were just beginning to assume a healthy complexion for the first time since the laying of the foundation stone when one of the trustees absconded.

With him he took the funds.

One of its pastors was a man who started a crusade that had earned him the enmity of a newspaper editor, who came to the church during one service and sat just under the pulpit. Before that service was concluded the mentally deranged cleric had drawn a revolver and shot dead the newspaper editor before putting a bullet through his own head.

Californians have a tradition of easy tolerance towards firearms of all kinds. With the State's origins echoing to the roar of guns and whine of bullets this is not surprising. But a firearm in fingers that would have been more suitably employed turning the pages of a Bible was more than even tradition could accept without criticism.

Such happenings provided the twenty-year-old church with a curious and oddly ill-becoming history of crime and violence.

But in 1895 the loyal congregation was making a determined effort to help Mr. Gibbon live down his church's spectacular past. Some sent their children to his Normal School, and among those attending its classes was Blanche Lamont. She had no special friends, although several of the girls in her class had laughingly joked about a young man they called "Blanche's beau," who had upon occasion loaned her music and even books. But Blanche was not a young girl who considered herself in love.

On April 3rd she left her aunt's home as usual for the regular class at the Normal School. She was working to secure a certificate that would enable her to become a teacher of other pupils, and this seemed to be the limit of her girlish ambitions. She set off that morning at the usual hour, dressed in a blue gown over which she wore a short black coat. Her hat had flowers tricked around a shallow brim. There was little money in her purse. Enough to pay her trolley fare and to buy a light midday meal.

She spent the morning in class and then went to another building to attend a cookery demonstration. When this early attempt at a domestic science class closed in the afternoon she put on her coat and hat and started back to her aunt's home.

She did not arrive.

Tea was held back for her. So was the evening meal, but she did not return, and her aunt thought she might have been invited home by one of her classmates and would probably be at the prayer meeting to be held that night at the Baptist church. She set off fully expecting to meet her niece in church, but she was disappointed. She did not see Blanche's flowered hat among those filling the pews.

During the service a young man seated in front of Mrs. Noble turned round and, choosing his moment, whispered that he had brought a book he had promised to give Blanche that evening.

"I'm surprised she didn't come with you, Mrs. Noble," he said.

His name was Theodore Durrant, and Blanche's aunt knew him by sight. She made some excuse to cover her embarrassment and left after the meeting without collecting the book for her niece. By this time she was genuinely worried. When she arrived home she burst into tears. Her niece had not returned during her absence.

She and her husband had little sleep that night, and the next morning Blanche's uncle went to the Normal School, where he was told that the girl had left the previous day at the usual time, about half-past three. Mr. Noble returned home and tried to console his wife with the suggestion that perhaps the girl had spent a night at some friend's home and would return later.

Somehow he didn't sound convincing, least of all to himself.

When another night had passed with no word from the girl Mr. Noble went to the police. The detectives he spoke to were not unaccustomed to fond parents reporting errant children staying away from home. Moreover, experience had made them cynical. When a girl of Blanche Lamont's age and looks stayed away from home the cause was usually dressed in a pair of pants. But they did not put it quite so crudely to the plainly disturbed uncle. One of them, named Anthony, said he would make inquiries, and with that Mr. Noble had to return to his wife, feeling far from satisfied.

Detective Anthony arrived at the Nobles' home, questioned the aunt and uncle and then Maud, and asked permission to go through Blanche's personal belongings. He expected to find some letters which could provide a clue to her disappearance, but he drew blank. There was no indication that the girl had been in debt or frightened of anyone.

Maud told him her sister had three rings.

"One was a garnet ring," she explained, "which I had exchanged with one of hers, a plain gold ring with a little diamond chip in the centre, and another stone ring."

Detective Anthony sent descriptions to the San Francisco pawnshops, but none of the three rings had been handed across a pawnshop's counter. The detective sought out Minnie Edwards, who usually travelled by trolley with Blanche.

Minnie agreed that she had gone to the trolley stop with her friend, but while they stood there a young man they knew came up.

"His name's Theodore Durrant," she told Anthony, "and he told us he had been waiting outside the school for Blanche to come out, and I judged by his manner that he wanted to see her alone. I felt that two was company and three none, so I took the next street-car and left them together. I noticed that they followed in the next trailer, and I thought he was going to escort her home. I can't say where they got off or where they went. I left the car at my own corner and didn't think to look."

Anthony wrote this down and kept his thoughts to himself. A man, it was always a man that made the little darlings leave home!

Minnie Edwards added that Durrant was the young man some of the girls talked of as "Blanche's beau."

"He seemed interested in her," she said archly, "or so we thought, and I heard her speak of him several times."

Two other pupils from the church's Normal School admitted seeing Blanche at the trolley stop with Durrant, and said that both had apparently been laughing and amused at something.

Anthony called on the Durrants. The family lived in the same neighbourhood as the Nobles, and the son was studying to become a doctor. He was of medium height, rather sallow in complexion, clean-shaven, and had eyes with a stare that had been described to Anthony as glassy. He was a friend of the organist at the Emmanuel Baptist Church, George King, and was generally liked by those who knew him and by the Baptist minister, Mr. Gibbon.

When Theodore Durrant was told by Anthony that he seemed to be the last person known to have seen the missing girl the young man appeared interested. He was certainly willing to talk about the absent Blanche, whom he claimed to like and even to admire, although he laughingly disclaimed being in any sense her "beau." He saw her at church and had sometimes talked to her after service, and they had some tastes in common.

Which was all very well as far as it went, but then he suddenly denied being on a trolley with the girl.

"Anybody who said they saw me must be mistaken," he told Anthony. "I was in class at the Cooper Medical School until four-thirty, so I couldn't have been."

He said he had gone to see his friend George King.

"You got any idea where Blanche Lamont might be?" Anthony asked.

"Not the slightest," said the young man with a shrug. "There was no reason why she should confide in me."

Anthony came away from the Durrant home impressed by the son's bearing and frankness. The detective knew it was not impossible for schoolgirls to make a mistake, and one young man could look like another. But Anthony went ahead with his inquiry, checking any facts he could come by.

He was interested when a man named Martin Quinlan said he remembered April 3rd because it was a Wednesday. That was the day he had seen young Durrant, whom he recognized, inside a street-car that was travelling along Bartlett Street.

"He was with a young girl," he told Anthony, and when shown a description of Blanche Lamont that had been prepared for the San Francisco newspapers he agreed that the young girl he had seen was dressed like the girl in the notice. Confirmation was provided by Mrs. Leak, whose house was almost opposite the high-steepled Baptist church.

When Detective Anthony reached her house in his quest for information she told the plainclothes man, "I saw Theodore Durrant go into the church on the day of Miss Lamont's disappearance, with a young girl whom I did not know, but who answered to the description that has been given out. I know Durrant well by sight, and he is always running in and out of the church. I didn't think it strange that he and a young girl should be entering it together. It is the centre of many local activities, and young people are often there on some business or other."

Anthony got this down in his notebook and then questioned Mrs. Leak further. He learned that she had seen Durrant and the unknown girl enter the churchyard by the gate in a fence beyond what she called "the walk," and they used a side-door. She hadn't seen them reappear. She had been expecting her daughter to arrive home and thought the time was about twenty past four. She added something Anthony carefully noted down. Durrant apparently had to grow persuasive to get the girl to enter the church with him. She had appeared to hesitate and even to hang back a little, so that he had caught her by the arm.

When Anthony approached the organist George King agreed that Durrant had been in the church around the time mentioned by Mrs. Leak, but he thought it was actually a little later, and perhaps ten to five would be more accurate. That was when he himself entered the room where Sunday school classes were held and began to practise the Easter music on the piano. He had detected a sharp smell of gas, and thinking it came from the library he opened the door and looked in, but could not trace a gas leak. He added that both he and Theodore Durrant had a key to the library.

He had returned to the piano and again began playing. His next words were taken down carefully by the attentive Anthony:

"I had not played more than a dozen bars when the door burst open and Durrant staggered into the room. His jacket and hat were missing and he looked awful. His face was deathly pale and bathed in sweat, and his hair was in disorder. There was a strange expression on his face which I had never seen before. I was alarmed and asked him if he were ill.

"He said that he had been at the top of the church, fitting the electric wires, that the gas was escaping terribly, and that it had almost overcome him. He asked me to get him a bromo seltzer from the drug store at the corner of Twenty-second Street and Valencia, which I did. We went into the church kitchen, where I mixed the bromo seltzer and he drank it off. It seemed to revive him and he asked me to help him carry down a small organ from the church loft to the vestry. I did so, though it would not be needed until Easter for the children's service. He complained of being

tired and said, 'I am all used up on account of that con-
founded gas.' We left the church together after that, and
Durrant accompanied me to my own door. He seemed better
then."

The organist had seen nothing of Blanche Lamont and
Durrant had not mentioned her name to him. He told Anthony
he was surprised that the smell of gas had upset Durrant. It was
not bad enough to make him feel queasy when he accompanied
Durrant to the loft.

Theodore Durrant had some questions to answer.

When they were put to him he was as unruffled as before,
and expanded his former admission. This time he admitted
seeing Blanche on the morning of April 3rd. He had met her on
her way to school and asked her to accompany him to George
King's home, but she had said that would make her late, so he
walked with her to the school door. This, of course, had no
real bearing on Anthony's inquiry. But Durrant next denied
entering the church around twenty past four with the girl. He
said he arrived at the church twenty minutes after that time,
but George King was not there. He had been made ill by the
escaping gas and had asked his friend to get him something to
make him feel better. He arrived home about six-thirty, and
after supper went to the prayer meeting. He said categorically,
"I was not on the Bartlett Street car at any time that day with
Blanche Lamont, and if she visited the church at all that
evening it was not with me."

Anthony left the Durrant house feeling dissatisfied, but
unable to do anything about it. He had for the time being come
to a full-stop.

But not Theodore Durrant, as events proved. After the
second visit by the police he began telling his friends he thought
the girl was in voluntary hiding, and that she must have her
reasons. He even informed Mrs. Noble when he met her at
church that on that memorable Wednesday morning her niece

had told him she was "tired of a humdrum life and might suddenly leave it all and go away."

"That's quite unlike Blanche," Mrs. Noble exclaimed.

To which he retorted, "I don't think Blanche wants to come back. I'm afraid she's unwilling to give up the life she's leading," but this kind of dubious innuendo was vigorously denied by Mrs. Noble.

However, she later admitted that it was possible Blanche had eloped. Why not? It was the recurring dream of a great many gently nurtured females in the late nineteenth century. Only, she referred to the possibility as contracting a secret marriage. Perhaps that sounded even more romantic. As she told one friend, that was greatly preferable to thinking Blanche dead.

Meantime the police had made inquiries of the Lamonts in Dillon, Montana. They were quite bewildered by their daughter's strange and unaccountable disappearance, and could tell the police of no one who had been communicating with Blanche before she went south to California with her sister Maud.

The case was beginning to accumulate some social dust when reaction came from Minnie Williams, who had been a friend of Blanche's. She became angry when she heard Theodore Durrant smugly voicing his gratuitous opinion that the sly, quiet ones, as he called them, were often the worst. Minnie took him to task. After he had gone, looking rather shamefaced, she turned to the group he had left and said spiritedly, "Blanche was as good and pure as any girl could be, and Durrant is only spreading these reports because he knows something of her disappearance."

If that were true, Durrant's contumely boomeranged, for Minnie's words were reported to Detective Anthony, who was back making inquiries after learning that a pawnbroker had been offered Blanche's three rings some five days after she had disappeared. The pawnbroker had not been happy about them, and the man who had produced them quickly pocketed the rings and went elsewhere. Another pawnbroker accepted them. Both pawnbrokers' descriptions of the man with the rings fitted Theodore Durrant, but before Anthony could approach the young medical student the rings were redeemed, according to the bemused pawnbroker by the young man who had pledged them.

On the Saturday before Easter Sunday the rings arrived at the Nobles' home, wrapped in newspaper, with no explanatory note, in an envelope on which the address was printed. When Mrs. Noble saw the familiar little rings she collapsed. Her doctor was summoned, and then the police.

Did the arrival of the rings mean Blanche was alive? Or was that what someone wanted the Nobles and the police to believe?

Before these questions could be answered Blanche's staunch friend Minnie Williams, a fair-haired lively girl of eighteen, had also disappeared. Life had not been easy for her due to the constant quarrelling of her selfish parents. She had left home to fend for herself and lived in Alameda with a friend. Just before Easter she took the ferry to San Francisco to stay with a Mrs. Voy. That evening there was a Young People's meeting at the house of a Dr. Vogel, who lived not far from the Emmanuel Baptist Church. But Minnie did not arrive at Dr. Vogel's and she did not return to Mrs. Voy's. When the friend in Alameda was contacted, and she reported that Minnie had not returned to her, the police were informed.

The two missing girls had been friends, and both had been associated with the Baptist church with the dominant steeple.

The ugly stories that had once been told about the church were revived. The Reverend Mr. Gibbon became a very harassed and unhappy minister. The ladies assembled to decorate his church with Easter blooms were also unhappy. They met in the vestry to discuss the floral decorations and a couple stepped into the library. A minute later there was a wild shriek. Minnie Williams had been found.

Her clothes had been torn from her body, her face was horribly distorted, and she had been strangled in brutal fashion. Her blood smeared carpets and walls. Fingernails had been buried in her flesh. Her torn clothing was flung about, and one garment had been forced down her throat with a stick. The tendons and arteries of her wrists had been slashed with a blunt-edged weapon, and ghastly wounds appeared on her bared breasts. Indeed a blunt knife was embedded in the right.

The discovery shocked San Francisco. The police were moved to put a strong guard on the church for fear a mob would break in during the night. From nowhere the rumour had spread that Blanche Lamont's body was also in the ill-fated church.

Waiting for day to break the now heavily committed San Francisco police force soon uncovered the fact that before leaving to go to Dr. Vogel's on the Friday night Minnie Williams had received a letter from Theodore Durrant in which he asked her to make an appointment to see him.

Dr. Vogel told the police Durrant did not arrive at the Young People's meeting until it was on the point of closing, at nine-thirty. He had been pale and his face was bathed in sweat as he asked permission to wash. He was gone some minutes, and when he returned appeared to be his usual assured self.

By morning the police knew Minnie had been murdered in a little room off the Baptist church's library and her nude and bleeding body dragged to the larger room.

Why?

Detectives again called at the Durrant home, to be informed that the medical student had left without saying where he was going. But the police were ready to uncover a large number of stones. They approached Durrant's sister and she told them he might be found with the U.S. Signal Corps at Mount Diavolo. The police left the Durrant home with a suit Durrant was known to have worn on the Friday. It was free of bloodstains, but in a pocket they found a woman's purse containing a book of ferry tickets to and from Alameda. The purse was proved to belong to Minnie Williams.

By ten o'clock on Easter Sunday morning a great crowd was gathered outside the Baptist church in Bartlett Street. Then the police arrived with a janitor who unlocked the door to the steeple. The rest of the church premises had been searched before dark the previous evening. The plain-clothes men mounted the steeple stairs in single file. These wound in semi-darkness to a space just under the eaves, where a pale object was found. It was the nude body of Blanche Lamont. She had died in agony, and her body had been brutally treated similarly to her friend's. But the curious feature was that her head had been placed on a wooden block, so that at first glance she gave the appearance of a corpse laid out for a lesson in anatomy in a medical school.

Her clothes did not turn up for several days. Whoever had killed her by slow strangulation had taken them and concealed them in the most unlikely nooks and crannies of the church.

When news of the discovery of Blanche Lamont's body was released San Francisco was in uproar. Nothing like this savage crime had been known in the gaudy history of a city that had been weaned on violence in many forms. This was senseless, brutal, obscene, and depraved.

Somewhere a sex maniac was at large.

Few hesitated to put a name to the murderer, and the hunt for Theodore Durrant was a wild and outraged hue and cry. The police understood they had to find him before some of the more militant citizens of San Francisco or there would be a lynching.

The police were moving in top gear. They found their man, on the road between Walnut Creek and Mount Diavolo. His old acquaintance Detective Anthony went to collect him. When detective and prisoner reached the ferry landing on their way back they were met by a mob shouting obscenities to the handcuffed young man.

Durrant managed a strained grin.

"They're howling for my blood now," he told Anthony. "But I'm an innocent man, and they'll be cheering and chairing me when the trial's over."

Theodore Durrant's pose, so self-assured and studiously controlled, broke when in prison, where his nights were made almost unendurable by a series of terrifying nightmares. It took medical science to calm a nerve that had been shattered and a will that had crumbled.

When questioned in detail he admitted arriving late at Dr. Vogel's, but claimed he had left home late and hurried, which was why he had been perspiring. The woman's purse found in his suit had been found on the path at the side of the Vogel's house. He had not written to the girl to meet him.

As to this last, the letter was never found, but of course it might have been the first thing a murderer would destroy when he had the opportunity.

The trial was marked by the prisoner's electing to go on the witness stand. He was dressed like a dandy in a neat black jacket and vest, with pale grey trousers. In the buttonhole of his coat each day he wore a fresh pink carnation, and he insisted on smiling on every conceivable occasion.

His family is said to have become paupers to raise the necessary funds to try to save his neck.

His fantastic performance in the court-room did little to repay their self-sacrifice. The prosecution went for him with all the old-style declamatory mode of oratory for which the American courts of the period were noted, and when he preened himself on the witness stand he was deliberately bullied and badgered.

As if that ordeal were not enough he was taken with the

jury to visit the scenes of the horrible murders in the Baptist church. He was compelled to stand on the carpet in the little room off the library that had been soaked with Minnie Williams' blood. He complied in a quite unperturbed manner.

Then he was taken up the winding stairs of the gloomy and dusty steeple, to where the body of Blanche Lamont had lain undiscovered for some three weeks. He appeared quite unmoved, while some of the members of the jury were heard to bite back moans.

Back in the court-room the defence tried a bold but amazingly unscrupulous move. It attempted to establish that the Baptist minister, Mr. Gibbon, had more opportunity to commit the crimes and easier access to the various regions of the church building. The defence even went so far as to intimate that the minister's conduct could be considered strange in the circumstances without enlarging as to how or why. It could do nothing in the matter of motive.

But then nor could the prosecution.

Blanche Lamont had not been sexually assaulted, Minnie Williams had. Blanche Lamont's body could be said to have been secreted away, for it had been pushed into a niche that had caused much bruising to the naked flesh. Minnie Williams' badly treated body had been dragged from a small room into a larger one and left there.

Such a different treatment raised all kinds of possible explanations. But to San Francisco, and beyond the city to the other cities and towns of the American continent, all explanations and queries merged in one final formula—Theodore Durrant was a sex murderer.

Ergo anything was possible and anything acceptable as proof, however much parts of it might be at variance with one another.

The prosecution not unnaturally took the precaution of having the prisoner tried for one crime only, the murder of Blanche Lamont. Had the defence won Durrant would promptly have been arrested and charged with the murder of Minnie Williams. But no citizen of San Francisco reading the newspaper reports of the dragged-out trial believed that Durrant was, in sober truth, being tried for only one murder. Else why take the jury to the little room leading from the church library?

What seemed to register was that Durrant had brutally murdered Blanche Lamont, possibly for what today is called "kicks," and had tried to get rid of her body in a way that offended everyone's sense of decorum and good taste. He had murdered Minnie Williams in a state of near-panic because Blanche's friend had a free tongue and came to the missing girl's defence. After that his panic had been complete.

He had not recovered his nerve until he ran away.

All this must have been clear enough to that San Francisco jury for they took only twenty minutes to reach a verdict of murder in the first degree, which carried a statutory penalty of hanging.

When the death sentence was passed he wilted very visibly. Only the pink carnation remained its perky self.

There was a united attempt by his family to have the court's verdict altered, but by that time too many unsavoury details about the medical student and his vicious past sex life were being made public, as well as stories of other women who had known him and disappeared, including a lovely redskin girl. There were several stays of execution, but soon after Christmas 1897 Theodore Durrant realized he had emulated his pioneer forebears by coming to the end of his own particular and personal trail.

On January 7th in the new year he mounted the scaffold shortly before noon. As late as ten forty that morning a telegram from Washington announced that the Supreme Court of the United States would not intervene to change the course of justice.

He died with a palpable lie in his mouth.

Just before plummeting into eternity he said bombastically, "If any man thinks I'm going to spring a sensation I'm not—unless it is a sensation that I'm an innocent man brought to my death by my persecutors. But I forgive them all. I forgive everyone who has persecuted me, an innocent man, whose hands have never been stained with blood, and I go to meet my God with forgiveness for all men."

Somehow he managed to make even his own earthly exit unnecessarily obscene.

★ 8 ★

The Case of the Early Burial

O<small>N</small> a bright June day a trap jogged along a dusty Irish lane and the fluffy clouds in the blue Cork sky threw occasional shadows ahead of the high-stepping pony. But there were no shadows in the mind or heart of young Effie Skinner as she glanced around her and stole a glance every now and again at the square stubbly face of the man holding the reins.

She considered she had full reason for being happy. She was changing her post for a better one. She had been contented as governess to the Caulfield children, but the prospect of life at Shandy Hall was vastly more appealing.

True, six children might prove a handful, but she liked children and her limited experience led her to believe that children liked her.

She was twenty and took herself rather seriously. Or perhaps it was her work as governess she took seriously, for sometimes she wondered if she could be two people. The straight-faced and strait-laced governess was only one Effie Skinner. There was another, a more secret Effie Skinner, who liked fluffy clouds and hedgerow scents and gay dresses that made men turn their heads.

By men she meant her conception of gentlemen, for to Effie Skinner the world seemed to be divided into two broad classes of people, those who soiled their hands with hard work and those who didn't. She had managed to become one of those who didn't, but she had a close-cherished desire to become a person who didn't have to work at all.

Such an ambition for a young woman like Effie Skinner in that year of 1886, when the Victorian Age was shortly to be stamped with the hallmark of a jubilee year, was only to be achieved by one legitimate means. Matrimony.

Because she was a creature of her own age she did not consider bearing and rearing six children as work, and perhaps she had a point strongly supporting her outlook. Whatever such work entailed, it was made immeasurably lighter by the employment of skivvies below stairs and Effie Skinner and her kind above. The skivvies were dirt cheap, as would seem to be appropriate in a well-adjusted world, and the Effie Skinners cheap enough.

Which is why daydreams were a continuing fashion for young women with slender means. It was a fashion a certain Charles Garvice was to capitalize on, and he was to have a legion of imitators. Their descendants in line of fashionable feminine fiction are still with us, though the fashion has had a few ugly crimps taken in it.

The trap turned through the gate that led along the curving drive to the front door of Shandy Hall, a rather diluted name for a somewhat diluted property, for the present occupant had lived most of his life as an army medical officer in India and somehow couldn't settle comfortably to an existence without chotah-pegs and punkah-wallahs. As a consequence he was accepted by the local gentry in that corner of County Cork with some reserve.

His wife, a pallid, timid-seeming woman without colour or sparkle, lived in his shadow, which did nothing to induce roses to bloom in her cheeks.

Mrs. Cross devoted herself to the singularly unexciting career of being a dutiful wife to her husband Philip. Not that her devotion was appreciated by him or understood. Indeed, he found her to be even more tiresome as the mother of six than she had been as the mother of five. Tiresomeness in Victorian domestic broodmares was a progressive quality, like self-centred indulgence in Victorian domestic stallions. However a benign Nature saw to it that they tended to overproduce and so thinned their own blood line.

Philip Cross's certainly needed thinning. The man was something of an anachronism even at that time.

He was sixty-two and thought of himself as thirty years younger. Well, men in all ages have been guilty of similar pieces of self-deception. But in the case of Philip Cross, who as a medical man should have known better, the deception was complete.

As the advent of Effie Skinner proved.

It is possible that he had thought little about his wife employing the young woman who had been a governess in the Caulfield family. The Caulfields also lived in Dripsey, not a great distance from Shandy Hall, and Philip Cross might have seen the girl in church from time to time without giving her a second glance.

However, when she took her hat and coat off in Shandy Hall, fluffed out her wavy hair, and smiled as she allowed her rather large eyes to light up, then Philip Cross found he had time for many glances.

At first they were furtive. Then less furtive. Eventually they became openly interested and even encouraging.

By which time the Cross children had taken to the new arrival, which pleased Mrs. Cross because their mother was encouraged to believe she had made a wise choice in offering employment to Miss Skinner before she packed her bags and left Dripsey.

Indeed, the coming of Effie Skinner was a major event in the life of Mrs. Cross. She had someone else to manage, even someone to talk to when she felt the need for feminine company she could accept on her own terms. What she didn't know, and couldn't even begin to suspect, was that Miss Skinner's advent was also a major event in the life of her husband.

Philip Cross spent hours in his study thinking more and more about his children's governess.

And about the years ahead.

Because he was a vain man and incapable of challenging his own fancies, he imagined the coming of the bright-eyed Effie Skinner with her fresh complexion and trim waist and ankles was some kind of test he had to undergo. To fail, all he had to do was ignore the young woman and not hover about the house and grounds looking for her.

Such failure was not attractive when the alternative was spiced with a sense of adventure and even possibly of fulfilment. This last was important to the master of Shandy Hall.

He felt his years were being wasted living the life that had become a stale habit and a dull routine. He told himself he had little to look forward to, he might even consider himself buried alive in that corner of Cork. Buried alive was a conception that frequently exercised imaginative minds in those days. And it would be unfair to Philip Cross to consider him unimaginative. He had a most lively imagination when it came to what he deemed best for Philip Cross, but in that he was not unique. Most genuinely selfish people share a quality that is really a defect.

However, sitting in his study and welcoming lecherous thoughts about the new governess was very different from doing something about those thoughts. Philip Cross was not notable as a man of action. He would always spend longer talking about a deed than performing it.

Which was probably a psychological safeguard.

But if he was to do anything about Effie Skinner, if he was to get anywhere with her, he had to start performing. Safeguards were merely hindrances.

So one day he chose his time carefully and caught the governess on the stairs, slipped an arm around that trim waist, and pushed his own trim whiskers into her young face. Then he really did feel thirty years younger.

He could even believe his feelings. Simply because Effie Skinner did not cry out in alarm and make a fuss that would bring Mrs. Cross hurrying to the scene on the stairs. It is possible that Effie had been compelled to accept similar robust masculine salutations in her previous career. She may even have lost a job because she had screamed in such a situation, for Victorian wives with dalliance-minded husbands were accustomed to remove the incitement to dalliance before doing anything else.

Things are very different today. But then property values have changed out of recognition. In the marriage mart as in those other markets where cash decided whether a deal is on or off.

So Effie Skinner stood her master's ground on the stairs and when he released her made sure he had reason to feel not only welcome, but excited and even invited.

She could have arranged to avoid him. Surrounded by six Irish youngsters nothing could have been simpler. Still pursued, she could have left. Instead, she remained at Shandy Hall, and as one would say today, she knew the score. Of course she could have protested when she was snared furtively and subjected to more whisker tickling, she very possibly did, but without anything that could be described as success, so perhaps success of that kind was less sought than success of another, which she certainly achieved.

Philip Cross became infatuated with her.

Possibly Effie Skinner played a game of amorous poker with rare instinct, which can be better than skill when one is only twenty.

Anyway, she was a colleen to supplant the wistful and over-pliant Mrs. Cross in the mind of Mrs. Cross's husband. Philip Cross told himself, and undoubtedly he told Effie, that he was in love with her.

He acted like it, and his actions became more and more demanding. So much so that the clandestine affair was discovered. The timid Mrs. Cross suddenly assumed the semblance of a tigress.

"You have seduced my husband, you wretched girl," she accused Effie Skinner. "You will pack your things and leave, and you need not expect a reference from me."

There may have been an overture of sorts from Philip Cross, but if there was he had to make it from a very insecure position and nothing he said changed his wife's rigid intention to have the young woman out of Shandy Hall.

So Effie Skinner packed her bags and prepared to take another journey in the pony-trap. But before she left Philip Cross sought her out.

He was effusive and he was compelling. He assured her that he would look after her.

"I'm not going to let you suffer," he said. "I'm going to take care of you."

He told her he had plans.

Perhaps if he had shared them with her he might never have seen Effie Skinner again. Because he kept them to himself he not only saw her, he married her in one of London's most fashionable churches.

However, he did tell her that he had already made arrangements for her to put up in Dublin. She could not stay in County Cork or the story would leak out and there would be a scandal. That had to be avoided.

In Dublin things would be different. He could come and see her there.

"And don't worry your head about money," he reminded her. "I'll attend to everything."

So Effie Skinner left Shandy Hall while there was still colour on the hedgerows and in the fields. She did not take with her a reference, but she did have a Dublin address, and when she arrived there she found Dr. Philip Cross had in one respect been a man of his word. She was expected and installed with no delay and no questions.

Winter came, and in the new year Dr. Cross suddenly found business matters demanded his presence in Dublin. He began to travel frequently to the city, and volunteered no explanation to his wife, who was curious, but who had to allow her curiosity to feed on itself. She realized that she had to be grateful for having salvaged her life from possible ruin, and perhaps because she had lived with Philip Cross the years she had she also realized that it was sensible to leave well alone.

However that may be, Mrs. Cross entered a period when her husband was travelling almost regularly from Shandy Hall to keep these unexplained business appointments in Dublin.

The business he had to attend was of course confined to enjoying illicit hours with Effie Skinner, who had become his mistress. A few months of scurrying antics, and he began to feel his age, which was distinctly annoying. If he could regularize his relationship with Effie life would be vastly more pleasant, but that was obviously impossible while he continued to be the husband of the Mrs. Cross who was mistress of Shandy Hall.

There was only one way to bring about a change.

He faced up to that just as he had faced up to the need for accosting Effie on the stairs.

Mrs. Cross quite suddenly became ill. She had to take to her bed, her body racked with fever, a feeling of nausea making her very weak. Her husband treated her, and her recovery was rapid. She still felt weak, but chatted about the coming of spring, when she would be able to go for walks in the fresh air. She was sure that would do her good. Her husband gravely agreed and encouraged her optimism.

Whether that was callous or kind, in the exceptional circumstances, it is hard to be sure, but perhaps one should give what credit may be due to a man who has had so many hard things deservedly said about him as Dr. Philip Cross.

His wife would not take those spring walks. She would be under the turf, not on it, and it was his intention to ensure that she arrived in her grave with all dispatch consistent with his own security.

As a murderer he had all the advantages of his professional training. He employed them unscrupulously.

When the mysterious malady returned he told his wife it was a bout of typhoid fever.

"Just a slight attack," he informed her. "I'll have Godfrey come in and look at you. Best to be on the safe side."

Dr. Godfrey was his cousin, and considerably younger than Philip Cross. When he arrived at Shandy Hall he was received patronizingly, practically told what the patient was suffering from, what to tell her, and what to do about the illness. The younger man, anxious to ingratiate himself with an older member of the family, accepted the assortment of cues given him and performed just as Philip Cross wanted him to.

The breezy Dr. Godfrey diagnosed typhoid fever, reassured the patient, and endorsed the husband's treatment for her. Dr. Godfrey might have been a broth of a boy at delivering a young Mick or Maggie in the small hours when the mother was having a hard time in a dark corner of a damp cottage where poultry roosted on the window sill, but he didn't know typhoid fever from a hole in a bog.

And it would be surprising if he hadn't realized as much when he left Shandy Hall that 24th of May, 1887. But a young man with a career to make wasn't prepared to argue with an experienced ex-army medical officer like Philip Cross.

Which was why Philip Cross had summoned him.

After Dr. Godfrey had left, the Caulfields called to inquire after the patient. Effie Skinner's former employers were informed by the man whose mistress she had become that there was unfortunately no change for the better.

After the Caulfields came the local minister, the Reverend Mr. Hayes, only to learn that his timing was poor, for the patient had just dropped off into a deep sleep and could on no account be disturbed. He too took his departure.

A week passed. Mrs. Cross became weaker, and this time she did not rally. Indeed, it would have been a miracle of chemistry if she had, for she was being systematically fed arsenic.

It was early in the morning of June 2nd that Mary Buckly, one of the Shandy Hall servants, woke up with the sound of someone screaming ringing in her shocked ears. She sat up, listening, but the sound seemed choked off. Mary Buckly had been brought up on a mental diet of leprechauns and little people. She did what her mother had told her to do in such circumstances. She put her head under the bedclothes and kept it there. She fell asleep, only to be terrified afresh by a banging on her door.

It was the master, and she heard him calling.

"Mary, wake up. I want some help. Your mistress is dead."

Mary Buckly rose and donned her clothes and was surprised at the brisk and businesslike manner of the man who had summoned her. Philip Cross did not act like a man freshly bereaved, but more like a released prisoner. He sat down and made out a death certificate for Laura Cross himself. He partook of a normal breakfast and afterwards sent a servant for the undertaker, who came and was told to provide for a most modest interment.

Philip Cross was no slouch when it came to disposing of his dead wife's body. She was buried in a cheap coffin at the incredibly early hour of six o'clock in the morning of June 4th. Most of the dead woman's friends who expected to attend her funeral were shocked to find the ceremony over.

There was a good deal of outraged comment upon Philip Cross's unseemly haste among the good folk of Dripsey, though a few friends pointed out that he had spent a good many years in India, where the climate was such it accustomed one to rapid burials. The balance of opinion remained distinctly critical, however, which did not faze the widower.

Two days after the early burial he brought his personal diary up to date in his own succinct style when he wrote in it:

> "Mary Laura Cross departed this life, 2nd. May she
> go to heaven is my prayer.
> "Buried on 4th.
> "6th. For Laura's funeral etc., five guineas."

Then he started to make arrangements for his imminent departure from Shandy Hall. The children had to be left in some responsible person's care, and he apparently had no idea when he would be back. He thought he might be going to England.

He was both glib and offhand.

Then he was off to Dublin, where he helped Effie Skinner choose the first things for her trousseau. For Effie's earlier dream was coming true. She was going to obtain security and status by marriage. She had allowed herself to become the mistress of a man old enough to be her grandfather, but who was behaving like a young blade with buck fever. She knew Mrs. Cross had died, and was surprised that she had caught typhoid fever, but the disease was a threat in those less hygienic days and a good many death certificates bore the two tragic words.

Effie did her best not to think of Mrs. Cross, and her best was amazingly sufficient, especially when she gave her mind to the serious business of trousseau buying with Philip Cross's money.

The pair took the steamer to England and in due course arrived in London. They stepped into a world that was like a fairy realm to the young woman from Ireland. The shops, the bustle, the people, the crowding social excitements all left her dizzy with delight.

She was swept up the aisle of St. James's, Piccadilly, and when she came down it she was Mrs. Cross. Philip Cross was no longer an adulterer or a widower. He was respectably married and about to enjoy his second honeymoon.

Laura Cross had been dead just two weeks.

Exactly a year before Effie Skinner had arrived at Shandy Hall with her luggage in the pony trap.

However, it is possible that Philip Cross, borne along on a wave of ecstatic enthusiasm for the highly dangerous course he had chosen to follow, overlooked an important detail. His wedding in such a fashionable church as St. James's, Piccadilly, was reported in the magazines devoted to town topics and society snippets, and such journals were read even more avidly on the far side of the St. George's Channel than in England.

The marriage became bitter news in Dripsey.

One of Philip Cross's relatives, alarmed by some of the criticisms he had overheard, wrote to the newly married doctor in London. He explained that Effie Skinner, as Dripsey folk still referred to the new Mrs. Philip Cross, would have no reputation left to come home to unless their return was fairly speedy.

He sounded genuinely worried, and the recipient of the letter, trying to read between the lines, decided there might be good cause when everything was considered. The wise thing to do seemed to be to return and confound the critics. It should not be too difficult.

He told Effie they were going home.

She appeared fearful, for a strict diet of lotus had given her mental indigestion.

"Do we have to go back to Ireland?" she said pleadingly.

"I have to consider my practice," her husband told her gently.

She had forgotten he was a doctor. That, however, was an oversight that would be rectified in the most startling and sensational fashion, sufficient to ensure that Effie never forgot again for the remainder of her life.

The return to Shandy Hall was a cold-blooded affair. The servants did their best to put on a show of welcome, but the neighbours obstinately remained absent. At other times they held aloof from the doctor and his new wife. Dr. and Mrs. Cross became virtual prisoners in Shandy Hall.

One curious outcome of the bold return was a shift in the direction in which voiced criticism was turned. While they had been in England the bitterest tongues had wagged about Effie. Now they wagged about her husband.

The change in direction was accompanied by a change in emphasis, and this was sufficient to perturb Inspector Tyacke of the Royal Irish Constabulary when he heard of the early burial of the first Mrs. Cross. He felt compelled to call on the local coroner for Dripsey, who told him there had been no post-mortem as a qualified doctor had signed the death certificate.

"Who was it?" the inspector inquired.

The coroner gave him an odd look.

"Dr. Philip Cross," he told the policeman.

"Cross himself!" Tyacke exclaimed. "Now I must make some inquiries. You may even be seeing me coming back."

"I won't act surprised," the coroner said grimly.

Tyacke called on several people who had been friends with Cross and his first wife. What they told him certainly sounded alarming. In fact, the Caulfields were almost vehement in their demand for an exhumation.

The inspector finished his local inquiry with a conviction that he had no other course but to apply for an exhumation order from the local magistrate. It was agreed to with some show of surprise, for Philip Cross still had considerable social standing as a professional man with an honourable career behind him. When Tyacke left with the order he returned to the coroner and handed it over.

"Here it is," he said. "You'd better make arrangements for an inquest."

The body that had been hurried to its resting-place was within a few hours exhumed and taken to the local mortuary. Tyacke was moving fast because he wanted something on the record. Philip Cross, a man showing restrained anger and some repugnance at this invasion of his former wife's final rest, turned up at the inquest. He sat alone.

There were no shocks or sensations. Tyacke was too shrewd to move without full knowledge of the truth. That way he could stumble over a legal obstacle.

The inquest was formally adjourned until a date set by the coroner. The cheap coffin was removed and behind the scenes a pathologist went to work on the contents of the dead woman's stomach. Back at Shandy Hall the man who had made almost laconic entries in his diary about his wife's death and burial sat alone in his study. He had changed from the ebullient and effervescing lover who had trod the fairy meads with his bride on their London honeymoon. He was locked in himself. Effie couldn't reach him, and she became scared and felt a growing presentiment of disaster.

It was a bad waiting time for both, but only the young wife showed how bad.

Not that showing her feelings earned her any sympathy from those who watched avidly for any sign of reaction or remorse in the occupants of Shandy Hall. The entire countryside became impatient for the inquest to be resumed. The newspapers hinted at frightening disclosures. County Cork shivered in an atmosphere of gathering suspense.

The day before the inquest was resumed Tyacke appeared at Shandy Hall. When he left he was accompanied by Philip Cross. He was taken to Cork, and charged with murder. The next day the inquest produced medical evidence to show that Laura Cross had not died of typhoid fever, as her death certificate attested, but from arsenical poisoning.

She had been murdered.

Cross had to remain in custody until the next Munster

Assizes opened. It was on the 14th of December that he appeared in the dock to answer the charge of wife murder. He
was a man who had already lost the first round in his fight
with the prosecution. His counsel had made a vigorous plea for
the hearing to be held in Dublin, where there was no strong
flow of local feeling and opinion against the doctor from
Dripsey.

The request had been denied.

The Irish Attorney-General entered the lists and led for
the Crown, and within a very short time Philip Cross had lost
another round to his embattled opponents. It was trenchantly
pointed out to the jury that a doctor who had spent as long in
India as Philip Cross could not possibly have been mistaken in
the symptoms of typhoid fever. So it could be presumed with
every assurance that the prisoner had deliberately lied for his
own reasons.

Those reasons, according to the prosecution, were very
obvious and it produced Inspector Tyacke to show how obvious
and how incriminating.

Tyacke took the witness stand and gave the evidence he
had obtained from the manager of the Dublin hotel where
Effie Skinner and Philip Cross had lived as man and wife when
Cross registered their names as Mr. and Mrs. Osborne.

It was stated that this Mr. Osborne had arrived at the hotel
with a large valise bearing PX in white on the side. The hotel
boots had been intrigued by the letters. for he couldn't see
how they could be anyone's initials.

PX, Tyacke told the intrigued court, stood for Philip Cross.

The Royal Irish Constabulary inspector had been thorough.
He had found a chemist who had sold white arsenic to a man
of Philip Cross's appearance, and he had induced the prisoner's
sister to admit that her brother had asked her to destroy some
old medicine bottles, but she had not done so. The bottles were
not to be found, but they had contained a white powder.

The post-mortem had produced a quantity of arsenic in the

dead Laura Cross amounting to 3.2 grains, and it was apparent that the poison had been fed to her systematically for months. According to the chemist who sold it, his customer had explained that he needed the arsenic for making a sheep dip.

Four days Philip Cross remained in the dock, while his life was wrangled over, and hourly he could see the growing hopelessness of his counsel's task.

After the foreman of the jury had pronounced the prisoner guilty Cross sprang to his feet and began a fiercely delivered explanation of why he could not have been responsible for the arsenic found in his wife's stomach.

Mr. Justice Murphy heard him out with a show of distaste, and then informed the hard-breathing prisoner that he agreed with the jury's finding. He lost no further time in passing sentence of death.

Philip Cross did not have to wait long in the condemned cell. On the 10th of January, 1888, a man in his mid-sixties stepped out of that cell to stand under the gallows. There was one very noticeable change in him.

His hair was quite white. Rumour claimed that the change had occurred in the space of the previous night.

★ 9 ★

The Case of the Open Grave

On the last day of November, 1946, Walter Coombs turned
along Slines Oak Road on his way home. The light was fading,
but with the leaves off the trees enough filtered down to make
walking easy, although the road is not a wide one and it had
a tendency to wind on its route from the Surrey village of
Woldingham to the cross-country road B 269 which runs from
Croydon to Limpsfield and on across the A 25 into Kent.

Slines Oak Road turns right off the B 269 not far past the
village of Chelsham, and Mr. Coombs had walked along it as
far as the chalk-pit, where the road curved, when he chanced
to look down at the pale blur of the escarpment. He caught a
glimpse of what appeared to be a loosely tied bundle of rags.
That would not have surprised him unduly, for all manner of
discarded objects found their way from time to time over the
pit rims of the various hillside declivities in the neighbourhood.

But there was something about the shape of the bundle that
made his step slow. He turned for a closer look, and it was then
that he knew what had struck him as odd and even arresting
about the bundle of rags. It had a shape, and the shape was
human.

In fact, the bundle of rags was a man.

Obviously this was a matter for the police to investigate,

and when Mr. Coombs had told of his discovery a constable named Hearn started back with him to the chalk-pit. They climbed down, smearing their clothes with light-coloured mud, for there had been heavy rains recently, and came to the body. Walter Coombs saw why he had thought at first it was a bundle. It was, as it were, bundled together compactly inside an overcoat, but now they were close he could see the length of rope that was secured around the dead man's neck and trailed away from the body like a twisted antenna.

Moreover, what had helped the illusion of being bundled up was the fact that someone had tried to bury the body in the overcoat. Not with much success, however, but quite obviously an attempt had been made to dig a grave, although the grave-digger had been discouraged after scraping no more than a shallow depression in the chalky ground. The tool used to scrape out the shallow grave lay near the body.

It was a pickaxe.

The points of it were caked with the chalky mud that smeared the clothes of the corpse and the two curious men bending over it. They might well be curious, because it did not require an expert to determine that the man in this open grave was the victim of violence.

For one thing, he had not walked to the site and started to dig his own grave before growing tired of such a dismal undertaking and committing suicide. He couldn't have. The soles of his shoes were clean. So someone, or possibly more than one person, had carried him.

For another thing, Constable Hearn had unbuttoned the overcoat on the body and found a green rag and another length of rope around the dead man's neck. When he leaned closer he could detect a smell of polish on the rag. Conforming to this abundance of materials wrapping the throat was the appearance of the face above it. Constable Hearn had no doubt that the man in the open grave had been strangled.

Which meant he had been murdered.

Also, that the person or persons who had carried him to the chalk-pit site and scratched the shallow grave had done so to lose a body that was a considerable encumbrance. But for some reason he or they had scamped the job.

Detective-Sergeant Cox agreed with the constable, and a telephone call was made to Dr. Eric Gardner, who was consulting pathologist to Weybridge Hospital. He arrived and climbed down into the muddy pit to make a first-hand examination before the body was removed.

His findings were rather expected. The dead man had died of strangulation, and the body had been dumped in the open grave prior to rigor mortis setting in. This could mean that the man had been dead only six hours, perhaps less, when someone began wielding the pickaxe down in the chalk-pit. However, the state of the body yielded even more helpful information. Rigor mortis was showing signs of wearing off in a few areas of the body. This could imply that the time of death had been around forty-eight hours before.

The body was taken to the public mortuary at Oxted, close by Woldingham, and there Dr. Gardner, aided by Dr. Keith Simpson the Home Office pathologist, performed a post-mortem that confirmed the original theory that death had been caused by the rope around the dead man's neck having been drawn tight enough to induce asphyxia.

A minor puzzling feature was that the corpse showed signs of having been at some time around death in a state of suspension. Yet there was no obvious indication that the victim had been deliberately hanged or even strangled to death by hanging.

It appeared to the two medical experts as far more likely that the dead man had been tied up and was prone on his back when he was strangled by the rope being drawn tight enough to choke him to death.

Not that death had come rapidly. Strangulation had been slow and coldly deliberate, and signs of haemorrhage on the surface of the victim's heart and lungs pointed to this, and in support was the evidence of the dark fluid distending the chest.

There was even evidence to suggest that, apart from being slowly brought to the point of an agonizing death, the murdered man had been handled with excessive savagery after being tied up, even tortured. He had suffered severe concussion from heavy head blows, and there was noticeable haemorrhage in the stomach and congestion of the intestines, the result of a heavy pounding of the body. Two ribs were fractured and muscles torn.

The dead man had been the victim of a most brutal and quite obviously deliberate attack.

But there was nothing in the clothes taken from the body to give the victim of such brutality a name. Detectives began making inquiries in the area around Woldingham, for the shallowness of that open grave and the discarded pick suggested that the person or persons disposing of the corpse might have been interrupted while down in the chalk-pit. Their activities, in short, may have been observed.

A couple of landscape gardeners, Fred Smith and Cliff Tamplin, had on the afternoon of the 27th noticed a man standing on the chalk-pit's bank. The time had been between four-thirty and four-fifty, as near as they could remember. They came walking down the road and the man standing by the chalk-pit heard them, turned and stared in their direction, then started running.

Surprised, they stared after him, and saw that he ran to the cover of some low trees. Behind the trees was a parked car. The man jumped in, started up the engine in great haste, and sped out on to the road and past the two gardeners on their way home from work.

They pulled aside as the car hurled past them, the tyres spinning stones from the road surface. The driver's face was no more than a pale blur, but they recognized the fast-travelling car as a Ford Eight. In the poor light at that time in the after-

noon it was not possible to decide in a few speeding seconds whether the car was dark blue or black.

Nor could they catch the registration number, though they were agreed that it most likely had the figures 101 in it. They were afforded that one quick look while the car sped towards a bend about thirty yards away, and then it had gone in the dusk.

This evidence provided something quite the opposite of what the police expected. Had the man by the chalk-pit been seen on the 28th or 29th, it might reasonably have been inferred that he had been there to take part in trying to conceal the body of the strangled man.

But from the times established by the medical experts Wednesday the 27th was the day before the murder was committed. What could be the implication?

The police decided that the furtive stranger in the Ford Eight had been inspecting a site for the eventual disposal of a victim who had yet to be killed. All in all, it was a fairly cold-blooded affair, streaked with plenty of what is legally termed malice afforethought.

The dead man, as events established, did not prove difficult to identify, and the Surrey detectives who made inquiries were exceedingly quick in establishing that he was a John McMain Mudie, who had worked as a barman at the Reigate Hill Hotel, just outside the Surrey town on the main road through Sutton to Brighton.

When the police came making inquiries Mudie was considered missing by the hotel manager. That is to say, he had left the hotel on the 28th of November and had not returned. But he had said nothing about going elsewhere. His spare clothes were hanging up in a cupboard in his room, his personal things were in the drawers of a chest. There was no sign of his having packed a bag ready to walk out on his job. Further, the other members of the hotel staff had no reason for recalling that he had acted in any way different from his normal self on the 28th or the few days earlier in that week. The hotel manager liked him and told the police he was a young man one took to readily, open and frank and with a pleasant personality.

Well, someone had objected to that pleasant personality.

The detectives who went through Mudie's effects found tangible evidence that the young barman had known three men, one of whom had been well-known in Australia as the Honourable Thomas Ley, the New South Wales Minister of Justice. He seemed a most curious person for the dead barman to have known at all intimately.

Ley was a colourful person. He was not ashamed of having lifted himself literally from the gutter, for after leaving school he had begun an incredible career in the most humble way, by selling newspapers. But he had been alert and ambitious, and spent long hours studying the law. He had done well enough to secure a clerical post with a firm of Sydney lawyers, and continued his studies until he had passed his law examinations and was accepted as a partner in the firm. Most men would have been content to go steadily from there. Not Thomas Ley, who appeared to be driven onward by some internal demon. He turned to State politics, and very soon became actively engaged in campaigning for the party of his choice. His political work brought him new contacts. One was a lawyer who specialized in promoting new companies and arranging mergers. It was highly profitable. Ley joined him as a partner.

A great volume of water had flowed under Sydney Bridge since then, but Ley forged ahead with his political activities, until he was the leader of the brash and noisy Progressive Party. He stood for the Hurstville constituency and won it by an overwhelming majority.

That was in 1917, with Australian troops dying in Europe and the Near East. Ley waved the Southern Cross to plenty of purpose. Four years after the close of hostilities, in 1922, he joined a coalition State Government and for his service was made Minister of Justice. He was forty-one, in his prime, a man who apparently need put no trammels on his political ambition. And so far as his term as Minister of Justice was concerned that was largely true, for he was a success. Even his opponents granted him that. But he overstepped an unseen line and wrecked his career.

He became too eager for early advancement, and saw no reason why he should wait in line for high office and quick preferment. He let his name go forward as a nominee for the Federal election and stood for Barton. Shortly afterwards his opponent withdrew from the contest, but changed his mind, and in the election lost to Ley. But there was some mystery about that withdrawal and the charge was made that he had been bribed to stand down.

Ley was named as the person who had offered the bribe.

The Australian High Court started an investigation into a case with a pungent smell. But the man who had been allegedly bribed by Ley had vanished, and was not available to give evidence, and so the case against Ley failed. Instead of this re-instating Ley in public favour it started a fresh rumour that Ley was responsible for having the man murdered, and even might have killed the man himself.

Ley composed himself, adopted a stiff-muscled look that was like a mask and continued as though nothing had happened. But something certainly happened to one of his business associates. The man was discovered dead at the bottom of a cliff.

Again the ugly rumours circulated. They did Ley no good at all, although there was no actual evidence to implicate him in foul play. But in 1929 Ley was existing on a series of bold bluffs and only just getting by when his share-pushing operations brought criticism from his political colleagues. Suddenly his political feet grew very cold. He packed his bags and came to Britain, where he established himself with a large bank balance. He was followed a short while later by Mrs. Maggie Brook, whom he had known for seven years, from the time when he became New South Wales Minister of Justice. When Mrs. Brook's husband, who had been a J.P. in Perth, Western Australia, died she allowed Ley to provide for herself and her small daughter. Mrs. Ley was seemingly not living with a husband with whom she remained on very friendly terms. She too came to England and frequently visited him in London.

It was all strangely cosy.

Such was a man who had been, apparently, on friendly terms with the murdered barman.

That part was wryly out of character.

But there were connecting threads. When the inquiring detectives found them they shaped up like this. Mrs. Brook's daughter was married in London and went to live with her husband in Homefield Road, Wimbledon. The house was divided into flats and the owner, Mrs. Blanche Evans, lived in one of them. In May 1946 John Mudie rented a furnished room in the house, and Mrs. Evans, a widow, liked the young barman and treated him as though he were her son. That was the month Mrs. Brook's daughter became ill and had to undergo an operation. Ley, who was an incurable busybody, interesting himself in other people's affairs, told Mrs. Brook that she should install herself in the Wimbledon flat and housekeep for her son-in-law. Why the suggestion was made has never been satisfactorily answered, but Ley was a man of curious mental impulses who could not brook being thwarted in his desires, and one fact is plain, the elderly Mrs. Brook, in her mid-sixties, was scared of him. Was it because she knew too much about his past and feared the time could come when he would resent the fact? It is at least possible.

But the truth is too much was possible with a man like Thomas Ley. He indulged fancies and obsessions to a point where he came dangerously close to behaving like a maniac.

Take for example his sudden switch of manner toward Mrs. Brook. She was at the Wimbledon flat because he had suggested it, and within a month he was accusing her of having an affair with her son-in-law. He told her as much on the phone at ten o'clock at night on June 12th. Then he rang up repeatedly to remind her that his mind had not changed. At two-thirty in the morning he arrived in a car and almost abducted her to Knightsbridge Court, his lease for which expired in a matter of hours, when he left to stay at the National Liberal Club while the bemused and thoroughly scared woman took up residence in a room in West Cromwell Road.

Some days later Ley again behaved most irrationally. He arrived in Homefield Road and informed Mrs. Evans that Mrs. Brook had phoned and requested him to take her away to avoid trouble with some men in the house. In a way it seemed plausible to Mrs. Evans, and when he asked who the men were she named three who lived in her Homefield Road house.

They were Mudie, Romer, and Wynn.

"Which one is Jack?" asked Ley.

"You must mean Mr. Mudie," she told him. "He is Jack."

Then Ley ceased being plausible by angrily suggesting Mrs. Brook had been to bed with this Jack Mudie. When Mrs. Evans refuted this and told him he was being objectionable and slanderous Ley slyly hinted that it might be one of the other male lodgers, but she resented this suggestion with equal firmness.

Ley left, but returned to say he felt he should apologize to Mudie, and he would like to meet him to make amends. She said Mudie had now left Wimbledon and was living at a hotel in Reigate where he was employed as barman.

When she closed her front door after Ley, Mrs. Evans thought she had heard the last of him. She was terribly mistaken.

Ley busied himself purchasing a property in Beaufort Gardens and having it turned into flats. While the conversion was under way Mrs. Brook's son-in-law received a phone call inviting him to tea with her at Beaufort Gardens, but he became suspicious because he did not recognize the caller's voice and did not go.

The detectives uncovering this tangled skein of events established that the young man's reluctance probably saved his life, for they proved that Ley had hired some thugs and was lying in wait for his arrival. Ley was apparently out of his mind with crazily induced jealousy that had no rational foundation.

That jealousy had to be appeased by violence because Ley was by this time a paranoiac. Where Mrs. Brook's son-in-law was fortunate Jack Mudie was soon to be dead out of luck, and all the words imply.

He became the elected martyr to be sacrificed to Thomas Ley's incurable jealousy which was eating at his sanity.

September came and Ley stayed at a Bloomsbury hotel where his wife was known. The head porter was Joseph Minden, and Ley put a strange question to him.

"Do you know of a man who owns a car and is capable of looking after himself?"

The head porter was very right to consider the request both strange and unusual. Cautiously he inquired if what Ley had in mind was something legal. Ley assured him warmly that it was and that the man could earn a good year's salary in a few weeks.

John William Buckingham owned a car and was known in Bloomsbury to undertake private-hire jobs. Ley, who had received the man's telephone number, rang him up and asked him to call round the next evening. When Buckingham arrived he was told a rigmarole about a couple of ladies who had been seduced by an unscrupulous character who was trying to blackmail them. Ley mentioned the name of another man concerned with doing something about the blackmailer. This other man was John Lawrence Smith, who was working on the conversion of the Beaufort Gardens property.

Ley had now contrived a web-like mesh of intrigue with himself and his well-lined pocket-book in the centre. When

Buckingham met Smith the plotter left the two men together, and Smith was primed to tell Buckingham that a mother and her daughter were the seduced women.

"They're being blackmailed now, while they're living in Wimbledon," he explained. He added that Ley was anxious to do something that would make the blackmailer cease annoying the women.

There were other meetings between Ley and the two men he wished to make his henchmen. There was much discussion, and Ley built up the lies and inflamed the other pair against an unknown barman named Jack Mudie. Lilian Bruce, who knew Buckingham, did not meet Ley, but she was employed to induce Mudie to leave Reigate and come to London. She was given a brand-new lie—namely, Mudie, a blackmailer, was wanted in London by Sir Edward Ley, a solicitor, to sign a legal document agreeing to cease annoying the two women she had heard about. Mrs. Bruce, like the head porter of the Bloomsbury hotel, wanted reassuring about this curious caper being legal and above board.

She was informed that Buckingham and Smith wouldn't be party to it if there was anything illegal about it. That was assurance enough.

Mrs. Bruce drove down to Reigate with Buckingham and his son on November 24th. They met Mudie in the bar where he was serving. Mrs. Bruce was most pleasant to him. The next day she arrived with Buckingham, but went into the bar where Mudie was serving on her own. She asked him if he would manage the bar for her at a cocktail party she was giving in London, and he said he would be delighted. She said she would give him a ring and make final arrangements.

On the phone she said she would pick him up in a car on the 28th. Mudie was waiting for her and he was driven to Beaufort Gardens. Thomas Ley's crazy lust was about to be sated.

By the time they had learned this much the police were ready to make a move. They arrested Ley, Buckingham, and

Smith. The three were charged with murder. On January 13th, 1944, the prisoners appeared in a line-up, and Cliff Tamplin, one of the two landscape gardeners, picked out Smith as the man he had seen standing looking down at the Woldingham chalk-pit. The police already knew that Smith had hired a car, paid for by Ley, for a week at a cost of twenty-nine pounds. The registration number of the hired car was FGP 101. It was a black Ford Eight.

The rest of the crazy quilt pattern of insane jealousy and senseless violence came out at the subsequent trial as a series of statements by the accused which led to fierce contests by opposing counsel, but in the main the facts resolved into a story of stupid subterfuge and blind hate in which others were trapped by their greed.

Only two of the trio stood in the Old Bailey dock, Ley and Smith, when the trial opened on March 19th, 1947, before Lord Goddard, the Lord Chief Justice. Buckingham had turned King's Evidence.

There was a story about some juggling with cheques, arranged by Ley to trap Mudie, who had indignantly sent the cheques back and avoided the trap. This was just another of the irrelevant asides in which Ley indulged himself from time to time.

Buckingham's evidence told of what happened at Beaufort Gardens when the decoyed Mudie arrived, expecting to walk into a colourful cocktail party. As soon as the street door closed on him a blanket was whipped over his head, and the barman was tied up by Smith and Buckingham, gagged, and carried down to a basement where he was placed in a chair waiting to receive him.

The two strongarm characters left the room and met Ley, who gave Buckingham two hundred one-pound notes, on the understanding Mrs. Bruce was to receive thirty.

"Go now and don't get in touch with me any more," Ley told Buckingham.

Smith was left with Ley.

On December 3rd Buckingham was told what had happened after he left Beaufort Gardens to pay Mrs. Bruce. Mudie had signed a confession, he was assured, and had received five hundred pounds and left England. Eleven days later Buckingham went to the Yard and made a voluntary statement to the police.

Smith's evidence filled in what happened after Buckingham walked out of the premises in Beaufort Gardens.

Mudie had been "bounced" along the corridor to the basement, where Buckingham had fallen on him, causing Mudie to mutter round his gag, "You're stifling me."

"You're breathing your last," Smith had told the trussed prisoner, but he tried to make the jury believe it was said as a joke. The prosecution returned to this point, and when challenged Smith changed that explanation to another. He had merely wanted to frighten Mudie.

Well, he very likely succeeded.

He said he left Mudie alone in the house with Ley after Buckingham had gone to find Mrs. Bruce, who was waiting for him in a nearby public-house. Afterwards Ley had told him things had gone according to plan and Mudie had been taken to Wimbledon.

When it came to Ley's turn to give his story he claimed he had not been in the house at Beaufort Gardens at all on the night Mudie died. He even insisted that he had never mentioned Mudie to Smith or Buckingham.

Someone was telling a very tall lie. The jury didn't have to strain very hard to decide who. But some of its members had to rub their eyes when the defence produced a curious witness named Robert Cruikshank, an ex-convict who said he had been in Australia in 1929 when Thomas Ley ran into political trouble and cleared off to England. Cruikshank claimed to have come from Switzerland by air in the afternoon of November 28th, apparently to bring a parcel of goods that were not declared

to the customs. The plane was privately chartered and Cruikshank claimed he had no idea where it had landed. He had
been met by a stranger waiting in a car and had been taken
direct to London to surrender the mysterious parcel. He was
to catch another plane back that night.

It sounded very like uninspired fiction.

However, in London he had time on his hands and went to
call on Ley. He admitted that he had never met Ley and did
not know the man, but insisted he had heard of him, knew he
was rich, and thought he had reason to suppose Ley would help
him get back to Australia. The fiction sounded even less inspired.

He arrived at Beaufort Gardens, though no one knows how
he acquired the address, about eight in the evening, and because the place appeared deserted he entered the basement,
the door to which was not locked. He used his cigarette lighter
to take a look around, and found himself staring at someone
tied up in a chair. The figure in the chair moaned just as the
fuel in the lighter gave out. In the dark Cruikshank felt his
way to the chair, tugged at the ropes binding the figure, and
then was stopped by the odd thought that this could be the
caretaker and an intruder was upstairs and might come back
and beat him up. So Cruikshank ended his story as no fiction
writer dare do—by walking out on the climax. But he did say
that, by tugging at the ropes, he might have killed the figure in
the chair.

That was too much for Lord Goddard, who felt constrained
to remind the witness that he had merely tugged on ropes
binding the man's arms and body. It was hardly the way to
strangle anyone.

It was a moment of sheer farce, but no one was amused,
least of all the grave-faced Lord Chief Justice. When it came
time to sum up Lord Goddard charged the jury, "When you go
to your room and consider the case you will remember, of
course, that you owe a duty and a grave duty to the prisoners.

But you owe an equally grave duty to the State and to the dead man. That man's life perished through some cruel and wicked act. If the evidence has brought home to these men, to your satisfaction, that they were guilty of that cruel murder it is your duty to say so, and if you are not satisfied it is your duty to acquit them."

The jury took less than an hour to decide it was satisfied that the men in the dock were responsible for conspiring to murder Jack Mudie and dispose of the body afterwards. After hearing their verdict Lord Goddard duly sentenced the guilty pair in the dock to death.

The appeals were heard during two days in April, but were dismissed and Mr. Justice Atkinson had a few scathing words to address to his listeners on the subject of Lord Goddard's alleged failure to direct the jury to consider the alternatives of suicide and manslaughter.

"The rope with a noose and slip knot must have been put deliberately on Mudie's neck," he said, "and had been pulled with such violence as to show the mark on the neck. There was therefore no obligation on the judge to direct the jury as to manslaughter. The suggestion of suicide is fantastic. How could a man tied up as Mudie was get a rope, tie it round his own neck, and pull it from behind?"

The question had no answer, as Constable Hearn realized when he stood with Walter Coombs in the chalky mud under Slines Oak Road one afternoon the previous November.

However, the suspicion that Ley was mentally unbalanced was supported when a panel of three alienists declared him to be criminally insane, and he had his sentence commuted to imprisonment in Broadmoor. Smith's was commuted to penal servitude for life.

Less than two months later Ley was dead. The boy from the gutter had climbed a long way, but he had fallen even farther.

⋆ 10 ⋆

The Case of the Scarlet Shroud

SHORTLY before the outbreak of the First World War the Paris police investigated a shooting incident in a flat in the Rue de Sèvres which they decided was suicide. However, there remained some sceptical folk who claimed they were not so easily satisfied as the detectives who called at No. 107 when they were summoned by the concierge.

It was March 5th, 1914, and there was a hint of early spring in the air, the last spring Paris was to enjoy before the world became convulsed in an armed struggle that was to bring changes that made the easy-going days of that March seem like a gentle lull before a tropic storm.

But not in the flat in the Rue de Sèvres.

There the detectives found Paul Jacques collapsed in a chair in the room kept as his study. A bullet had penetrated his right temple and the weapon from which the shot had been fired lay on the bloodstained carpet at his sprawled feet. The dead man was about twenty years older than his very distressed wife,who claimed that her maid Georgette Picourla had found the husband dead when she had taken him a cup of drinking chocolate. The police accepted this version of the discovery. It was not the truth. The discovery had been made not by the maid, who had been told by her mistress that Monsieur Jacques had shot himself, but—if it had been a discovery—by Madame

147

Jacques herself. Had the police known this they might have taken longer to decide the cause of death.

Certainly the maid had doubts, but then she felt she had reason, for some weeks before she had observed her mistress tip a white powder from a packet into a tureen of soup specially prepared for the husband. Without telling Madame Jacques, the maid informed the husband what she had seen. He had merely looked at her and nodded, but had taken a sample of the soup to a chemist he knew.

"I'd like this analysed—discreetly," he said.

The chemist looked at the soup and at his customer. "Certainly, monsieur," he agreed. Later he looked no more surprised when he informed Monsieur Jacques, "A corrosive sublimate. Possibly lethal."

Even Monsieur Jacques had not been surprised, but perhaps he knew that he lived in the shadow of death. He had not seemed to care very much, which says a good deal for the kind of life he had lived with his younger wife.

When he had met her she was Hera Myrtel, a convent-educated young woman of charm and obvious breeding, the daughter of a Lyons tradesman of wealth and standing. She had been born in 1868, reared gently until her father's business enterprise crashed. She went to Mexico, where at the age of twenty-four she captured the heart of an older man who was a silk merchant. She married Paul Jacques and returned to France with him. They settled in Paris, where their daughter Paule was born and the mother wrote romantic novels under her maiden name. Under the same name she published some verse. In time she gained a minor literary reputation, and because her husband had the money to indulge her whims and caprices she was able to establish a literary salon of sorts, where she met a number of the literary hangers-on to the coat-tails of those who have arrived. Quite a few were men, and some of them young and attractive and unscrupulous.

Hera Jacques found it a simple matter to indulge herself

with a whole series of lovers, who came like perching rooks, and disappeared the same way. If the silk merchant protested there is no record because any protest was utterly ineffective. Paul Jacques was indulgent to a degree that was almost morbid. It was as though his pen-wielding wife could crush him by a mere show of contempt.

So perhaps he did not object to death as an eventual way out of a sickening dilemma he had no way of solving while alive.

After the burial the widow made up her mind to go to Mexico in person to handle the intricacies of her late husband's estate. She arrived in due course in Mexico City and almost at once made the acquaintance of a Madame Laforce who lived in a large home along the ultra-smart Avenue de los Caballeros. As a new arrival from a Paris literary set the novelist and poetess was very welcome among the group of close friends encouraged and entertained by Madame Laforce. The group had a truly international complexion, and it was at such a gathering that Paul Jacques' handsome widow met for the first time a dark-faced man who smiled easily and had brown sad eyes. He said his name was Weissmann, but as though to endorse the Rumanian origin he claimed he had adopted the Balkan-sounding name of Bessarabo.

He has been described as a mystery man. He was accepted for what he purported to be, a European engaged in a world-wide timber trade, but he rarely referred to any activity that could be remotely connected with timber. He had money always available, his bank credit was good, and he had time on his hands.

Madame Jacques found him attractive, her daughter of eleven years did not. Bessarabo was not discouraged by the unconcealed dislike of another man's offspring from paying court to that man's widow. Madame Jacques could not truth-fully be said to have allowed herself to be swept off her feet. She was far too well adjusted and far-seeing. But she encouraged the Rumanian's suit, and presumably because her calculating mind had decided such a marriage would be to her advantage she agreed to change her status and name to that of Madame Bessarabo.

This was done in December.

Whereupon she decided the literary circles in Paris were again in need of her patronage and her shining example. Accordingly the family arrived in the French capital, were installed in a fashionable apartment, and Hera Bessarabo looked around her, prepared to pick up again the threads of her past life of indulgence and flattery.

However, there was something more than a short interval of time that marked a difference between the salon lioness that had been and the one that sought to be. Hera Bessarabo, ever on the qui-vive for fresh sensation and a vicarious thrill, had succumbed to the enchantment of hashish and the potent promises of a drug made from Mexican mescal. While no dope fiend, she was almost certainly a drug addict, and this had not improved a temper that had been noted hitherto for its volatile quality.

The Bessarabo household became a storm centre, and the storms blew up with tropic intensity and frequency. The man who had once been known as Weissmann learned the lesson that had brought sharp disillusion to Paul Jacques. It was on balance better to give way to his wife than oppose her wishes. On those occasions when some flickering spark of masculine dignity demanded that he stand up to her tantrums it was to hear her scream a particularly disturbing phrase.

"I'll have your skin!"

It has been said she used the threat repeatedly when thwarted by Paule's stepfather. What she meant by the phrase is not too clear. What it came to mean in the long term is all too horribly clear.

As it had been to Paul Jacques, who was comfortably out of such domestic disturbances, and whose ghost, had it a mind to return to once-known haunts, might have viewed with ironic appreciation the marital martyrdom of a man who professed to know a great deal about timber, but allowed his wife to treat him as though he were a wormy log.

Madame Bessarabo might have been under the influence of hashish when she first tried to administer physical punishment to her husband. He awoke one night to find she had her hands around his throat and was pressing with a passion not dictated by love. When he overcame her apparent determination to return to the veiled state of widowhood she broke into tears and pleaded that she was over-wrought.

The next time such a rage produced a similar state of being over-wrought she did not rely on her bare hands. She pointed a pistol at his head and shouted in Mexican Spanish, "Out of my way or I'll remove you." It was no idle boast. Almost before she had finished uttering the words she was squeezing the trigger under her finger.

Bessarabo had flung himself to the floor, thoroughly scared. He had every right to be. The bullet whistled through the space he had been occupying seconds before.

Firearms were no innovation in her life. Apart from the shooting that removed Paul Jacques from her life, there had been another violent episode in Mexico before she and Bessarabo had arrived at terms of intimacy. On that occasion also lead had sped from a gun. The real truth of the incident was about as well concealed as what really happened to her first husband. What was known was that she and her small daughter had gone to the home of a wealthy Mexican ranchero in the countryside. The Mexican had died of gun wounds, and his distressed visitor had told a story of four horsemen arriving and shooting her friend before riding off again. The way the story was told it sounded like a vengeance plot. For the second time the police had accepted her version of a fatal incident because no other was offered.

But the sudden strikers of vengeance were a theme she was to resort to later, thousands of miles distant from the Mexican rancho.

Bessarabo had a friend named Berlioz. One day he confided to this friend that he thought his wife would eventually treat him as she had the others, and left Berlioz to make what he would of the remark.

It was in February 1920 that she next got her hands clutched convulsively around his throat. Again her husband's masculine strength kept some air in his lungs. He decided it was high time to leave a woman whose fits of rage were apparently growing yearly more uncontrollable. Moreover, her daughter had grown up resembling her mother, in looks, in temperament, in all those unprepossessing qualities that her mother reserved for her life behind the closed doors of their home. But there was no chance of Bessarabo getting off a domestic hook.

"Walk out on me," his literary wife told him, "and I'll go to the police. I'll expose you."

The precise implication was never made clear, but it seemed to refer darkly to the manner in which the husband came by his wealth, so it can be assumed that the remark's origins were rooted in those first days in Mexico, when a man infatuated by a sophisticated Parisienne told her too many secrets when trying to impress her with his ability to keep her in that station to which she aspired.

Bessarabo remained on the hook. Uncomfortably on it.

Being a man with a temperament capable of compromise and accommodation, he sought to ameliorate his harsh lot by the unpublicized purchase of a property at Montmorency, where from time to time he found relaxation and retreat in the company of other women. One of this very close circle was his secretary, to whom he imparted his fear that his wife and stepdaughter might have a design for murdering him. His secretary didn't seem alarmed. She probably knew the boss and the kind of tales he told when the level in the cognac bottle was sinking.

Bearing that in mind, it is curious that to another of the

Montmorency mademoiselles he said that he might die if an enemy from his past found him.

There were occasions when he couldn't have been highly diverting as the great lover. Opportunity became appreciably less when Hera Bessarabo's keen nose ferreted out the love nest. But the secretary stayed around as an accommodating wench on her day off. Bessarabo even revealed a capacity for growing fond of her in his fashion.

A month after the latest hands-round-his-neck bid Hera Bessarabo received a letter postmarked Mexico City. The concierge took it up to her, saw the letter opened and read, and then was surprised to see the collapse of the hitherto self-contained and domineering Madame Bessarabo. The concierge picked up the letter, glanced at it, but couldn't read a word of the Spanish. That evening he heard a violent quarrel in the Bessarabo apartment. It was louder and more prolonged than usual.

For three days after that Bessarabo did not leave the apartment. When he stirred abroad he went in a hired car. At night he made a parade of locking doors and windows. According to the concierge he behaved like a man overcome by fear.

It took a few weeks for him to pluck up the nerve to whip his secretary off for a brief stay at the Montmorency villa. The change wrought an improvement in his condition. When he returned to Paris he was even able to joke with the concierge, who wondered much, especially as that morning another letter bearing a Mexico City postmark had arrived, and Madame Bessarabo had been overcome very much as before when she scanned the news in Spanish.

There followed another protracted quarrel. The concierge, now really agog with curiosity, stole up the stairs to eavesdrop, but was disappointed to hear Monsieur and Madame Bessarabo apparently slanging each other in a language he did not understand, but which he took to be Spanish.

That night the lights in the Bessarabo apartment remained burning until after day had dawned. But bright and early Madame Bessarabo was about and stirring briskly through the rooms, and a short while later she told the concierge she and her daughter were going to the country, and that she wanted him to carry down their trunk and then to call a taxi.

The concierge had to be helped in handling the large trunk he found awaiting him in their apartment by the mother and her daughter. Even so the trunk was bumped down most of the curving flight of stone stairs to street level. The concierge went to collect a taxi, and when he returned with one the Bessarabo apartment's females were waiting with two valises. They, their valises, and the trunk were loaded into the taxi, which drove away.

But that evening the women returned on foot. They were not exactly confiding, but apparently there had been a change of plans, and they were no longer willing to sojourn in the country.

In the following days Monsieur Bessarabo was not seen to be entering or leaving the apartment. A few friends were informed that he was away on business.

"I don't like it," the hired-car driver told the concierge.

His name was Croix and he looked it, a man who when crossed became belligerent, as he was now, and he thought with reason. Croix had driven Bessarabo around Paris for weeks and had been told never to be late when ordered. Bessarabo's *pourboires* had been generous, and Croix had grown to expect the sizeable tips. On July 30th he had deposited Bessarabo at the door of the apartment building and been given instructions to call in the morning at nine.

He had arrived, waited, and then sought the concierge to learn that the family was out, the women off to the country. When they had returned Croix came calling and was informed that Bessarabo was out of Paris.

After a few days he again made inquiries of the concierge.

"He's not back. No sign of him," said the man.

"I still don't like it," Croix insisted.

"What can one do?"

"There's the police."

The concierge made a sound that was not polite. But then the police was a subject most concierges were not prepared to be polite about. They fought a never-ending fight with local regulations supported by pin-pricking police action. However, Croix felt put out at losing his tips, and he was quite prepared to make trouble for someone to relieve his feelings, so he called at the police station in the Quartier Saint-Georges and delivered himself of the opinion that something had happened to Monsieur Bessarabo of 3 Square Bruyère.

With the complaint on the record, the local detectives went round to have words with the concierge, and shed their formal lassitude when they heard of the big and very heavy trunk. Such pieces of luggage are invariably suspect in inquiries where someone is missing after known quarrels. Moreover, the picture of life in the Bessarabo apartment as offered by the concierge was not one of domestic harmony. They tried to trace the trunk and started by trying to locate the taxi driver, which wasn't too difficult, only to learn from him that the trunk and his female passengers had been taken to the Gare du Nord, where he had left them.

The detectives tried to find a porter who had collected the big trunk and drew blank.

They went back to Square Bruyère to start again, this time by interviewing Madame Bessarabo. She had a tailored story to offer. It was true her husband had returned late at night as Croix had said, but he had spent most of his time in the apartment packing the large trunk. He had left the apartment early in the morning after telling her to meet him with the trunk at eleven o'clock at the Gare du Nord in time to catch a train for Montmorency. She remembered seeing him collect a large number of papers and documents from a drawer which he had always kept locked.

"Why are you taking those?" she had asked.

"I want to destroy them after reading them through," he had said without enlarging.

She had arrived at the Gare du Nord with her daughter and the trunk at about ten-thirty, for she wanted to be in good time. But her husband had not put in an appearance, and she had thought he had gone off with his secretary. She had taken her daughter to the Gare de Lyon, across the river, had lunch in the station restaurant, then returned to the Gare du Nord, where Bessarabo was pacing up and down. He told her his plans had changed. He had the trunk brought from where she had deposited it, put it in a taxi, and drove off with it after telling her he would be coming back.

She had waited for an hour, which was just as well if her story had any truth, for the taxi-driver who had collected her husband now returned with the trunk still in his cab. Her husband wanted her to send the trunk on to Nancy, the taxi driver said. So she had got into the cab and been driven to the Gare de l'Est, where she had put the trunk on an eastbound train and taken a third-class ticket to Nancy.

She had neither seen nor heard from her husband since that afternoon.

"I think," she finished her story, "he's gone off with his secretary, possibly to Rumania, where he was born."

The story was full of false touches, but this last was wellnigh more than the hard-grained Paris plainclothes cops could take without letting her see they thought she was a rare liar. But they trailed off to the Gare de l'Est, and sure enough such a large trunk had been sent on to Nancy. A form with the name Bessarabo on it was dug out of the receipt files. A clerk recalled the young woman who signed the form. She answered to the description of Paule Jacques, whose name had never been changed to her stepfather's.

But she had bought several yards of rubberized sheeting as well as a length of manilla rope on August 1st, the detectives found, after making inquiries in the shopping area the mother and daughter would patronize. On the 2nd Madame Bessarabo had presented to a notary what she claimed was a power of attorney, duly signed by her husband, authorizing her to be paid more than half a million francs which was due on July 31st to Bessarabo as commission on a very large oil deal.

The documents relating to the oil deal had been found among her husband's papers. They would have been valid if the deal had gone through, but it hadn't.

When this was explained to her, and she understood she couldn't collect the money, she became abusive.

What the detectives had found out was told to the local *juge d'instruction*. He authorized them to go to Nancy, where the trunk, still being held at the station against collection, was found and opened.

Inside was a man's body dressed in a scarlet flannel under-garment, like a gruesome shroud, which was bound to him as he remained in a sitting posture by a stout leather strap. It was impossible to say who the man was for his face had been beaten to a mask of pulp. Every feature had been destroyed. There was a bullet hole in the back of the terrible head.

The trunk which had been used as a portable coffin had been lined with rubberized sheeting.

Some hours later the corpse without a face, removed from its scarlet shroud, lay in a Paris morgue, and Madame Bessarabo was asked to take a look at it.

"This cannot be the body of my husband," she said very readily. "Monsieur Bessarabo was slimmer, younger in every way. This is the body of a fat man."

She was pressed for a more detailed statement and this time she said the letters from Mexico City had originated from members of a secret society who had decided her husband must die. Her husband had become frightened, and cleared out all the papers he had concerning the activities of this secret society to which he had belonged. It was the only addition to her previous very thin tale.

The shades of those four horseman at the rancho were on the the move. However, as a variant, it was not an improvement on the previous story that had satisfied the Mexican police. The Paris police had heard fanciful tales before. But their job was to find proof or establish lack of it, so they tracked down Mademoiselle Nollet, the very obliging secretary, only to be told she knew nothing and to hear her repeat it every time they tried a fresh question.

They found a boat attendant at Enghien who had rented a rowing boat to a couple of women who might have been Hera Bessarabo and her daughter. The women took two objects out in the boat, which might have been valises, but when they returned the boat was empty. The younger said her companion had been sick, but that could not account for the large quantity of water in the bottom of the boat, as though it had been shipped when the boat tipped as one or both had leaned over one side.

Because the boatman thought the younger looked like Paule Jacques the lake was dragged. The dragging was a waste of time. Back to Paris went detectives who were beginning to feel frustrated, and to think with good reason they had been led a wild-goose chase.

Madame Bessarabo received another call from them. The detectives had brought some fresh questions that required new answers. She hedged and said cannily if the dead man could possibly be her husband, then the person responsible for his murder was a Senor Becker, an enemy of her husband's in South America.

Now occurred one of those coincidences that happen outrageously in real life, but which no fiction writer dare aspire to—a man named Becker committed suicide in the Bois de

Boulogne a short while after Madame Bessarabo offered her latest titbit to the police. They tried desperately to link the dead Becker with the dead Bessarabo, but could prove no connection.

Belatedly, perhaps, the women in the flat in the Square Bruyère were arrested and lodged in the prison of Saint-Lazare. There the elder divested herself of a new statement. She said a letter from her husband's secretary had fallen from Bessarabo's pocket on the evening of July 30th, and when they quarrelled about it he struck her brutally. She had snatched up a gun to scare him into leaving her alone. It had gone off, and he had been wounded fatally.

Her stories showed no sign of improving!

She had told her daughter, when roused by the shooting, to go away. Paule had had nothing to do with the tragedy. She, her mother, had packed the squatting corpse in the trunk and sent it off to Nancy. All the girl had done was help get the trunk down from storage on the sixth floor.

At any rate this statement provided admission of shooting Bessarabo, but when the taxi driver who had picked up the trunk at the Gare du Nord was found, after a great search, he failed to recognize either of the two women.

Their trial opened at the Seine Assize Court on the 15th of February, 1921. It quickly became a wrangling match between histrionic advocates who were aware they strutted their small stage in a drenching limelight.

When the last piece of incredible drama seemed to have been wrung from the conflicting and often confusing evidence Paule Jacques sprung a surprise and brought the whole case to shuddering life again by interrupting the court when she rose and cried, "The truth. I have to proclaim the truth!"

There was silence save for a low moan from her mother, who slipped down in a faint.

The bench ordered the young woman to relieve herself of

the hidden truth with no further delay. Whereupon she began another incredible story. Her stepfather had been a brute. No woman had been safe from his lust. He had many times attempted to seduce her. Her mother had lived in terror of his rages and animalism. She told how she had run into the living-room after hearing the revolver shot.

"Oh, God," she had exclaimed, "what have you done, mother?"

"Go back to bed," Madame Bessarabo had ordered, and then added, "What has happened is only justice."

She had tried to argue with her mother, and remembered her saying, "It was his life or mine. Now go on back to bed and leave me alone."

She claimed she had wanted to call the police, but her mother had refused to allow this. All this time she hadn't seen the face of a figure that was covered by a sheet on which crimson stains were spreading. When she made to pull back the bloodstained sheet her mother had dragged her away, saying, "You must never know who it is. But believe me, Paule, it is not your stepfather. I can't tell you the awful secret of what happened here tonight."

The young woman in the dock had got this far with her related melodrama when her mother recovered, sat up, and in the natural pause following the last words cried, "*Calle te!*"

The sudden use of a Spanish command to be silent made the young woman break down. As she tried to control herself her mother again shouted in Spanish. The Bench ordered her to keep quiet or she would be removed. Paule continued with her story of how that night and during the next days her mother had kept her locked in her room until she was forced to type at dictation a formularized power of attorney and then handed a pen.

"Sign his name—Bessarabo," she was ordered. "His real name's Weissmann, and Bessarabo is false, so it won't be a forgery. You know he owes me the money, and you know he's gone off with that Nollet woman."

The taking of the roped trunk to the station was given a fresh version. The only point all versions had in common was the place of destination—Nancy.

Paule ended her interrupted outburst with the words, "That is the complete truth."

Her mother, some minutes later, was asked if she had anything to say. In those minutes a considerable change had overcome Madame Bessarabo. It was as though she had sunk back into herself, like a fighter who had lost the will to continue a bitter struggle.

She shook her head and said, "I have nothing to say except my daughter did what I told her to do. You must acquit her."

The muddled and untidy case finally was left with the jury, who had to decide on a verdict. The one they produced was guilty with extenuating circumstances.

That meant the guillotine would not be dragged from its corner and dusted off. It meant just as surely that the daughter would be freed.

Such was the case.

Paule had, as the cynical considered, bought her freedom by shopping her mother, who was sentenced to penal servitude for twenty years. She took the sentence with almost contemptuous composure. The younger woman looked at her in horror and became shriekingly hysterical.

Paris blinked, shrugged its shoulders, and quickly forgot the Bessarabos. Almost a year later to the day, on February 25th, 1922, it got a glimpse of Anatole Deibler's guillotine, when Henri-Désiré Landru, a real past-master at losing bodies, offered his neck to the shiny axe. But even he was unable to lose them all, even with the aid of his smelly furnace at Gambais, though he had a terrific run for his "fiancées'" money, all 275 of them according to the names listed in the little black book he threw from a taxi after his arrest.

He must have read the reports of the Bessarabo case while in jail. If his views could have been recorded they should have been interesting, even enlightening. But murderers on murderers may well continue to remain a theme that is offered no real scope in what used to be known as cold print.

★ 11 ★

The Case of the Bogus Baron

I<small>T</small> was shortly after Christmas that the dwellers in Andrew Street began remarking on the unsatisfactory state of the drains in the neighbourhood. Andrew Street was in the developing Melbourne suburb of Windsor, and by New Year 1893, which was a hot summer, the smell was bad enough for someone to go to the police.

"Where does the smell come from?" asked the station sergeant.

"It's spreading all over the neighbourhood now," he was told, "especially if there's any sort of breeze. But it seems to be worst around the Drovens' house. Perhaps it's because they've moved out."

The police sergeant was interested. He learned that the Drovens were a couple not long out from England. The man had told neighbours he was a toolmaker. The woman had said little enough. She was small and rather shy, with a quick rather shuddery smile, as though she were afraid to allow anyone to see she might wish to be pleased. A woman who had, so wagging tongues said, been afraid of her husband, a man with a sharp tongue and eyes that somehow seemed never to change expression. The menfolk of Andrew Street hadn't taken to him. As a cobber Droven was an unknown quantity. He did nothing to change his status, and on January 5th handed over the keys

163

of his Andrew Street house to the agent from whom he had procured them.

The police became even more interested when they heard of the violent quarrel in the Drovens' house late on Christmas Eve. The windows were closed, although it was a hot night, but still the shouting and screaming disturbed neighbours down the street.

One woman told a detective who came making inquiries that on the afternoon of Christmas Eve she had seen Mrs. Droven for a few moments in the garden.

"She looked terrible," the detective was told. "She had a black eye and she looked as though there were bruises on her face and neck. I just yelled across the fence to her and she ran indoors. Real scared."

The police called on the agents responsible for the letting of the house the Drovens had taken. They found the manager in charge of the office worried.

"There's certainly a smell," he agreed. "I've been hoping it would just go. It can't be the drains, for we had them tested before that English family moved in, and that wasn't so long ago."

"You've been along to the house yourself?" he was asked.

He admitted he hadn't had time.

"I hand the keys over to likely tenants who want a house in that district, and they go along and see for themselves. Trouble is the few who've been there just bring the keys back and say it won't suit them. A couple did mention the smell, but, as I say, I've been hoping it was just the hot weather and it would go the same way it came."

The police decided they had best borrow the keys and examine the house for themselves. When they entered it they had no need to go hunting a stench. It met them in the hall, and it was a close, fetid odour made worse by the close atmosphere of a house with all its windows closed in hot weather. The smell seemed worse in the living-room, where one of the flagstones forming the base of the hearth had at some time been removed and the space filled in with cement.

The detective in charge of the police decided the cement should be broken. He had a fair idea of what would be found under the smelly hearth. The cement was not thick. A few blows at the edges cracked it, and the kneeling police cleared away the jagged pieces to uncover the body of a young woman in her nightdress. She might have been pretty, but it was hard to say as her body was lifted out of its unusual grave, for a blow from some heavy weapon had smashed her skull, and her throat had been cut.

Her killer had made very sure she was dead.

The unwholesome discovery was removed from the house and the air of Andrew Street became sweeter for its residents to breathe. More detectives arrived at the empty house to search the rooms and examine the furniture that had been left. They came upon a large family Bible. The inscription on the fly-leaf informed them that it had once been the property of Mrs. Mather of Rainhill in Lancashire.

They found nothing else that could be considered a clue to the identity or whereabouts of the absent Mr. Droven. But they made it their business to cover every possibility that might inform them where he had headed when he left Andrew Street.

His trail was crossed by the dockside police. A man answering Droven's description had made inquiries about a passage to England. He had apparently gone to Sydney. The manhunt switched to New South Wales, and again a man answering the description of the wanted Droven was remembered.

But he had not used the name Droven. He had inquired about a passage to England, and had left Sydney. He had given his name as Baron Swanston.

There was no certainty that he had actually sailed, and the police were in some doubt as to whether Droven had been laying a trail to mislead them. Inquiries for the arrest of a man answering his description were sent to police throughout New South Wales and Victoria, and a cable was dispatched to England. Mrs. Mather of Rainhill should have some news.

So a curious manhunt was started in two places at the same time, twelve thousand miles apart, to discover anything that could be learned about a man who had posed as a bogus baron and probably could smash a woman's head and cut her throat without that noticeably fixed expression in his eyes changing.

In far-away Lancashire things happened with surprising swiftness. When detectives called on Mrs. Mather, who still lived in Rainhill, and mentioned a family Bible in which her name and address were inscribed, she pressed a hand quickly to her mouth and said in a choked voice, "Oh, don't say something's happened to Emily!"

The story came hesitantly.

Emily was her daughter and the Bible was one Mrs. Mather had given her before the young woman left for Australia with her husband. They had only recently been married.

Emily Mather had been starry-eyed when she married Albert Williams on a fresh autumn day. The date was the 22nd of September. Mrs. Mather's eyes grew moist as she recalled the wedding and her own mixed emotions at the time.

"I couldn't help worrying a little. Emily was so fresh, so untouched, and Albert was a man of the world. I prayed that she would be happy, that she had made the right choice for a husband."

Williams was a comparative newcomer to Rainhill. He had descended on the district some months before meeting Emily Mather, and had seemed a rather flashy individual in that quiet North Country town, which is about four miles from St. Helens and even today has only some six thousand inhabitants. He had rented a house in Lawton Road on a short-term lease, and made himself very approachable.

In fact, to anyone who would listen, he was prepared to relate his adventures and the story of his travels in such distant parts of the world as the United States, Australia, and South Africa. He would drop into one of the local hostelries and buy drinks in a somewhat patronizing way, which was resented even if the local brew was always acceptable.

He was a good-looking man, with fairish hair and clear complexion. Mrs. Mather put his age at around forty, which she had thought too old for a husband for her Emily, but the girl had been unable to resist the dashing figure cut by Albert Williams, with his fashionable flowing whiskers and London-cut clothes.

"He was really too old for Emily," the mother insisted, and then remembered her visitors were policemen. "But what has happened? Why are you asking these questions?"

"We've been asked to make inquiries, Mrs. Mather," she was told. "It's probably no more than a routine matter, but if there is any further news we shall call on you again."

When they left the modest house in Rainhill they knew the woman who had given her family Bible to her emigrating daughter was filled with foreboding. They had to make further inquiries in Rainhill, and what they learned elsewhere appeared to justify the anxiety entertained by Mrs. Mather for her daughter in Australia.

The detectives had a chat with a waitress in a local hotel. She told them that Bert Williams had spent a good deal of time bragging in the bar and showing other customers some stones he claimed were uncut diamonds. She once heard him talking of a fight he had with a pair of thugs who had set about him. If his story was to be credited, he had left the pair rolling on the ground and feeling grimly sorry for themselves.

"He talked big, he acted big," she said, "but I couldn't take to him. I didn't like the way he flashed his money, and the way he looked at me made me feel I wanted a bath."

On one occasion she had grown interested enough to ask the

bar lounger what he was and had been puzzled by his ready reply.

"An inspector of regiments, my dear."

Seemingly others in the town had been given the same information, and possibly because his listeners had no idea what an inspector of regiments was or did Williams had been constrained on at least one occasion to let them see for themselves, presumably believing that old con man's axiom that seeing is believing.

He had accordingly appeared on one occasion in the streets of Rainhill garbed in a uniform none of the inhabitants had seen before. It had been rather arresting, and indeed it should have. It was designed to be precisely that, for it was obtained from a theatrical costumier's in London, as diligent inquiry later proved. All in all, Albert Williams had gone to considerable trouble and not a little expense to dazzle the eyes of the Rainhill natives. He had descended on them like a being from another world.

To the worldy-wise detectives picking up the bits and scraps of news about him that must have been his intention.

What then of his purpose?

Well, he had given out to those he considered his new-found cronies that he was in the district on a house-hunting mission. His principal—whatever that was intended to imply—was a Colonel Brooks who wished to settle in the Rainhill area. The colonel had not visited Rainhill while Williams was there, and no one in the town had heard where the military gentleman resided or why he wished to come to that part of Lancashire, but it was in the name of Colonel Brooks that Williams made arrangements to lease a comfortable residence in Lawton Road.

This was Dinham Villa, where he installed himself, and left the interested neighbours to suppose he was making arrangements prior to the colonel's arrival. The villa had seven rooms and was a reasonably commodious Victorian dwelling, which Williams secured on a six months' lease at a rental of fifty pounds a year.

He had been anxious to have in the agreement a clause allowing the colonel to renew if he was satisfied with the villa as a home.

The house agent was very ready to promise there would be no obstacle to an extension of the short lease.

Whoever Albert Williams was he was a fake. The detectives had learned enough to establish that. They moved closer to scenes that had known him most intimately and arrived at Dinham Villa. Neighbours in Lawton Road and local tradesmen who had called at the villa while Williams was living there mentioned his married sister and her children. Apparently she had arrived quite suddenly with her four children and stayed with her brother for a week.

Williams had explained her not appearing in the town by the fact that she was resting before she started on a journey to America. She was going down to Plymouth, from where the ship in which she had booked berths sailed. Her husband was in California. The poor woman certainly had a considerable journey ahead of her, which made it appear strange that she should elect to come all the way up to Rainhill first, instead of going straight to Plymouth.

But at least that was in keeping with most facts learned about Albert Williams. They were strange. Inexplicably so.

The cautious inquiry he made of Dinham Villa's owner before he signed the six months' lease fell into the same category of strange facts. He had insisted the house agent give him her address, and when he called on her he was equally insistent that Colonel Brooks was a man seriously concerned about the level of the floors in any house he occupied.

"The colonel, dear lady," he had said as though such a foible did not require explaining, "is unable to live in a house with uneven floors. I am afraid he would not approve of the floors in the kitchen and scullery at Dinham Villa, which is otherwise most suitable, I assure you."

The villa's owner wondered whether the absent colonel was really more concerned about stone-paved floors being cold and damp in winter and muggy weather. Anxious not to lose a tenant who might renew for a considerable period if Williams was to be believed, she expressed herself as ready to have the kitchen and scullery of Dinham Villa refloored with cement.

So Williams had signed the lease in the colonel's name, and the fresh cement floors had been laid by Williams after he had taken occupancy of the villa.

In Dinham Villa the detectives stood in the kitchen and walked around the floor. The senior one stepped into the scullery and then returned with a frown on his face.

"We'll have to have them up," he said, "now we've come this far."

Following the example of the Melbourne police, the Lancashire police attacked an area of cement flooring that was less well-laid than the remainder of the area. When the news of what was happening leaked reporters arrived, by which time a crowd of Rainhill townsfolk had taken up positions outside the villa, agog to witness the comings and goings of the police.

Mrs. Mather was not one of them. She remained in her home very anxious to avoid the gentlemen of the Press.

Excitement stirred through the waiting crowd when a policeman wearing a shocked look left the villa, elbowed his way through the throng, and hurried to the nearest tobacconist's.

"I've been sent for some cigars," he told the shopkeeper. "The strongest you've got."

When he returned to the kitchen at Dinham Villa the cigars were handed out to the shirt-sleeved constables resting on their picks and shovels. The window was open to clear a noisome stench. It came from a patch of broken cement in the floor. The rubble had been pushed back until the cigars arrived.

Fortified with the cheap cigars, the diggers made fresh headway in prising up the cement their blows had cracked. They uncovered the crooked shape of a baby that had been strangled. Their other discoveries were less pleasant.

The woman was in her nightgown. Her long dark hair draped her face like weeds. The features under it were sufficiently preserved to suggest a photograph might be recognized. Her bosom was dark with a shiny breastplate of blood. Her throat had been cut.

The three other children were like the woman, who was presumably their mother, dressed in nightclothes. They too had had their throats cut.

The crowd outside Dinham Villa remained long after the diggers had gone and their discoveries had been removed. When the police photographs were circulated they brought a swift response from a couple of men who realized they were dragging a very shabby skelton out of a family cupboard.

They called on the police and said their name was Deeming.

The one who was spokesman for the pair added, "That woman found in the house at Rainhill. We think she's our brother Fred's wife. He married her twelve years ago, and we thought they were still living in Liverpool."

The third brother had been known as Mad Fred by his family. His full name was Frederick Bailey Deeming. He had married a dark-complexioned Welsh girl in Birkenhead in 1881. His brothers spent a long time at the police station explaining that the marriage of Mad Fred had been an unhappy one. The wife had done what she could for the sake of the children, but her husband had neither provided a decent home nor treated her with consideration.

"We talked to him once or twice," said the spokesman. "But it did no good. After all, there were the kids to think of, but Fred was no good. That's the truth of it. No good and thoroughly selfish and work-shy. That was our Fred."

Cables began to hum between England and Australia. The

story was a sensation in Europe and Down Under. For Deeming alias Williams alias Droven had vanished under his latest and most spectacular alias, the bogus Baron Swanston.

Before he was found and brought to trial a truly amazing career of fraud and violence was uncovered which extended around the globe. He had first deserted the wife he murdered in Rainhill when he set off for Australia in 1883. He was then about thirty. He had lived in Adelaide under the name of Ward before in 1888 sailing for St. Helena and defrauding two brothers on the trip of sixty pounds. He arrived with his family in Cape Town, and posing as manager of a diamond mine began to defraud various jewellers not only in that city, but in Johannesburg and Durban. He was remembered in Klerksdorp for a gold mine swindle that netted him nearly three thousand pounds before he fled with his family to Aden en route to England, where he blazed a fresh trial of frauds from Hull to London, back to Stockton, then shipped out to Australia before doubling in his tracks again to North Africa and once more returning to England.

In Yorkshire he had been a millionaire, in Belgium for a short period he was a nobleman named Dunn. In Montevideo they had had the good sense to arrest him. When he arrived in Melbourne on December 15th with Emily Mather he must have astonished the confiding English girl by putting in a claim to the owners of the ship by which they had travelled from England for compensation for the loss of a valuable necklace belong to his wife.

She was lucky to have a wedding ring, much less a valuable necklace.

Perhaps it was an outraged justice that ordained a woman should provide the snare that tripped his very agile feet and brought him retribution.

Her name was Katie Rounsfell.

She made his murderous acquaintance on a ship sailing from Melbourne to Sydney. The inquiries into sailing times for

England had been a bluff. So had a visit to a Melbourne matrimonial agency. If they were not bluff, then they revealed a most disturbed mental state, something that had not previously occurred to impair the manoeuvres and manipulations of Fred Deeming, the fast thinker, the fast talker, the very thoroughgoing throat-cutter.

On the voyage to Sydney she asked him where he was going. "To the goldfields," he said.

Well, there were all kinds of humans grubbing for the bright metal in the Australian bush. It did not seem unreasonable that a baron should be one of the motley crowd. In fact, Katie Rounsfell found she rather admired a man who might have lived soft most of his life suddenly stripping away the social veneer and using his muscles and working up a sweat. It suggested a will to succeed, and men who succeeded appealed to her. There were more than enough of the other kind to go round. Besides, Baron Swanston sounded impressive in ears that in the late nineteenth century might still—though somewhat diffidently—be termed colonial. Especially female ears, for after all there was plenty of legal precedent establishing that the feminine for baron was baroness, and Katie Rounsfell was entitled to her dreams just as surely as Effie Skinner a few years before.

In Sydney the bogus baron seemed not so prepared to be preoccupied with Katie as he had on shipboard. After all, he was back on terra firma and had to vanish, at least until he knew no hue and cry had been raised by a certain toolmaker named Droven.

When he met Katie he told her that he had secured a post with Fraser's mine, the fabulous Southern Cross. He was starting out at once, and she should come out and join him later.

It sounded like an invitation to the Australian girl. The bogus baron went off to the goldfields, and Katie Rounsfell daily thought more of joining her baron at the Southern Cross and perhaps becoming a baroness. She was still indulging her fancy, and had almost brought herself to the point of leaving Sydney, when the news of Emily Mather's body being found in Melbourne sent her hurrying to the police.

Her story was passed to Sergeant Considine, the Melbourne C.I.D. man in charge of the Australian end of the world-wide investigations. Considine had produced a thick dossier full of information about Frederick Bailey Deeming, and he had secret reports that the bodies of several women had been found in houses he had rented in Johannesburg. In fact, to date, Deeming was known to have been responsible for the deaths of six persons, two women and four children, and possibly for three or four more women.

Sergeant Considine thought Katie Rounsfell had had a narrow escape.

So did Katie Rounsfell when she was able to overcome the sense of shock and loss occasioned by the news she had read in the paper.

Considine wired the police in Bathurst. It was the bogus baron's turn to be shocked when reality caught up with him. He left his office one day to feel a hand on his shoulder and looked up into the face of a stranger.

"Baron Swanston?" the policeman asked.

"Yes. What is it?"

"I'm arresting you for the murder of Emily Williams at Windsor," said the stranger with the hard grip.

"Windsor?" the arrested man exclaimed. "I've never been there. How come you've grabbed me?"

"We'll learn later. If you're innocent you'll be released."

To which the bogus baron offered a very bogus retort. "Many an innocent man is hanged these days."

But the man who had arrested him didn't look specially upset by the news.

He was transported to Perth, where he had the good sense to perceive that the role of a titled gent could win him nothing but dislike and distrust after the deception he had practised.

"I'm Williams," he admitted to the Perth police. "But I didn't kill my wife Emily. That I swear."

This avowal might have carried more weight if the bodies under the cemented floors of the kitchen and scullery in Dinham Villa had not been uncovered and removed. When he arrived in a cell in Perth he still wore his moustache, of which he seemed to be quite proud in some foppish conception of nineteenth-century masculine good looks. But one morning it was missing, and he had no razor. It is believed he scraped the whiskers from his upper lip most painfully with a piece of broken glass. Probably to make recognition in Melbourne less certain.

Considine sent a detective named Cawsey to collect the man all Melbourne wished to see. Cawsey was not alone. He was accompanied by a man named Hirschfeldt, who had been found in Considine's police probe.

Hirschfeldt had been a passenger on the ship that brought Emily Mather and the man she had married from England to Australia. As soon as Cawsey's companion saw the prisoner he nodded excitedly.

"That is Bert, as his wife called him, and they were on the passenger list as Mr. and Mrs. O. A. Williams."

The arrest was cabled to England. A Scotland Yard senior detective took ship to Australia. If Baron Swanston or Bert Williams or Droven cheated justice by being found not guilty in Melbourne, then he would be extradited to Britain and charged with the murder of the dark-complexioned Welsh girl he had hauled around the world with their growing brood before he induced her to pose as his sister prior to cutting her throat and the throats of his three older children and strangling his baby.

The mills of the gods were beginning to grind exceeding small for Frederick Bailey Deeming.

However, the State of Victoria was jealous of its reputation.

Deeming would have to provide solid proof of his innocence if he was to keep his neck from a noose made of Australian hemp. The word monster for multiple murderers has been overdone to the point where it has wellnigh become meaningless, but somehow it still fits Deeming, three-quarters of a century after his name and photo were covering the front pages of the world's Press.

He thought he had one chance of winning sympathy in Australia, by keeping Katie on his side. So he wrote her a very indifferent letter, for the strange man of violence was practically illiterate, in which he stressed his innocence, and told her his feelings for her were unchanged and brought him comfort. He added his little piece, first recited at Fraser's mine, about innocent men being hanged, and then went to work in earnest by telling her if she would not marry him life would not be worth living. At the very end, after his scrawled signature, he made the request that she send him some money to help pay for his defence costs. If she hadn't any she might sell some rings he knew she had and send him the cash from the sale.

He was a real ball of fire when it came to telling people what they could do for him.

If he had been a public hero the crowds that gathered to meet his ship and train on the journey to Melbourne could not have been greater, except that the shouts held the wrong kind of enthusiasm and at least one crowd tried to lynch him. At Adelaide an elderly woman was so fascinated by her proximity to a man she was sure was a multiple murderer that she came back several times to stare at him as he sat at a train window. He became enraged and threw some whisky into her face.

In Melbourne fifty witnesses identified him. No one could deny the figure was impressive. It was established that he had at different times used fifteen aliases. Also an impressive figure.

When he saw that he had no chance to secure an acquittal by maintaining his innocence he attempted to demonstrate that he was insane. In court he assured the jury his parents had both been in an asylum and that was why he had been nicknamed Mad Fred. One of the doctors who attended him while in prison also had something to tell the jury.

He said, "Deeming frequently spoke of his dead mother, who, he declared, appeared before him every morning, and who during one of these appearances, while he was in Sydney, told him to kill every lady friend he had."

Before the jury retired he made a speech in his own defence, and he grew excessively abusive.

"I haven't had a fair trial," he ranted. "It's not the law that's trying me, but the Press. The case was prejudiced even before my arrival by the exhibition of photos in shop windows, and it was by means of these that I was identified. I leave it to the jury to say that it is not the case that there are hundreds of people in Melbourne who would execute me without a trial. If I could believe that I had committed the murder I would plead guilty rather than submit to the gaze of the people in this court —the ugliest race of people I have ever seen."

Australians never forgave him those last words.

He was found guilty and the jury added a rider that he was not insane. From stonewalling they had changed to really smiting the bowling.

He was sentenced to death, and the Privy Council in London refused a stay of execution. He was hanged on May 23rd, 1893, at the Swanston Jail, Melbourne.

The bogus baron must have flinched at such irony, which may be why he claimed to be Jack the Ripper, which was impossible. Deeming was known to have been in prison while the Ripper was carving the women of Whitechapel into obscene shreds.

⋆ 12 ⋆

The Case of the Empty Laundry

CLEAR that pile of earth away from over there," said the foreman to the couple of labourers. "We can get it out of the cellar later."

He had gone and left them to a cold draughty job. It was December and the big iron stove across the cellar was red with rust and giving out no heat. The two men wielding shovels worked hard to keep warm, and the only sound in the cellar was their heavy breathing and the scraping of the shovels along the stone floor until the blade of one struck some hard object with a dull sound.

"Hey, there's something under this dirt," said the man.

A few minutes later they had bared a large wooden packing case. It was heavy when they tried to move it from the nest of earth where it must have been for a long time, for the timbers were damp and half-rotted away.

"Let's see what's in it," decided the man who had found the packing case.

He aimed his sharp-edged shovel blade at the packing case and prised off some of the rotted slats. The two workmen looked inside and then at each other. The packing case contained an old leather trunk, patterned with mildew and damp patches of lime. It had been bound with leather straps, but the damp of the earth mound had rotted away the leather until a twist of a shovel blade would snap them.

The trunk's lid was thrown back, and a choking, tangy smell of lime made the finders of the trunk cough. At first glance it appeared that the trunk had been filled with pieces of leather and lime that had become damp and formed lumps, but crumbled to the touch.

They scraped away the top layer of lime and leather pieces and came upon something that ensured their work for the day was over.

It wasn't much later that Lieutenant William Belshaw hurried across Philadelphia to reach Kensington Avenue and the empty premises that had the name of the Red Star Laundry still over the entrance.

He had been told a couple of men shovelling dirt had found a body in the empty laundry. Well, experience had taught Bill Belshaw that it was always open season for hidden corpses, even less than two weeks before Christmas. The precise date was December 13th, 1915, and what the men in the laundry cellar had found would push some of the war news from Europe off the front page of the *Public Ledger*.

Belshaw went down into the cellar, now smelling of a strange blend of damp and lime and something he didn't want to put a name to, and after examining the mess the shovels had made of packing case and leather trunk decided that it had all better be removed for a detailed examination elsewhere. When the men from the morgue arrived with their ambulance he had them sheet over the entire pile of packing case and trunk with its contents and remove it to where Dr. Wadsworth, the medical examiner, could go to work on it without delay and without interruption.

What Dr. Wadsworth prised out of the crumbling trunk was virtually a skeleton that was fully dressed.

It took a good deal of expert and precise manoeuvring to get the once-human contents of the trunk laid out for examination on one of the morgue's chill slabs. The clothes attested to the corpse's sex—male: but they required a good deal of cleaning before one could be sure of colour and texture. The pervading dampness of the cellar's mound of earth had done a great deal of damage. The whole point of the earth mound, indeed, was to provide just that amount of dampness, which would make the lime active as a destroyer of flesh and fabric.

Dr. Wadsworth knew he was confronted by quite a task.

Bill Belshaw felt the same about the difficulties confronting him, for one cannot photograph a skeleton and expect recognition.

What the doctor established was that the corpse was that of a man about thirty-five years of age. He had had fair hair and had been slightly above medium height and of good stature. He had been in the trunk for at least eighteen months, possibly for two years. The cause of death was very quickly discovered. He gave the thirty-two bullet to Belshaw.

"As he didn't eat it, Bill, you've got a murder on your hands," he said laconically.

Which was no more than Belshaw had surmised. People who try to lose a body the way this one had been dumped always have an excellent reason. They also have a very justified fear of the police.

This case, Belshaw knew, wouldn't be the easiest in his career. In fact, he might require a lot of luck if it wasn't to be the case that spoiled his career, because he had to go back two years before he could begin. To help he had the few articles that had been buried in the trunk with the shot man.

Among them was a nail-cutter, some keys on a ring, a few coins, and two articles that seemed to him out of keeping. These were a prayer-book and a small crucifix. Dr. Wadsworth had also been able to decide that the dead man's suit had been tailored from dark blue worsted, and he had deciphered the tailor's name. It was the name of a firm in Walnut Street.

Of more immediate help to Bill Belshaw were the pieces of old leather used as filling for the trunk. He realized they had been used because they had been available when the corpse was stuffed into the trunk. He checked through the lists of persons reported missing in Philadelphia between eighteen months and two years before. That was where he came across the name of Daniel J. McNichol.

McNichol was a leather merchant who had premises in Hamilton Street. He had been reported as missing to the police on March 14th the previous year. In short, the report was twenty-one months old. The details handed in at the time of the report were not many, but they made the difference between a shadow and substance.

McNichol had been a little over thirty, which checked with the police surgeon's estimate of the age of the corpse. Anyway, there was no glaring disparity. McNichol had been the partner of a man named Edward Keller. Between them they ran the leather business.

Moreover, McNichol had been well known as a local footballer, and when he disappeared he had not long been married. His wife had previous to her marriage been Marie Jennings. She had given birth to the missing man's child a few months after the report that he was missing had been handed to the police department. Now the mother and her child were living with Mrs. Jennings, the wife's mother.

What Belshaw also found on the record was that there was a more recent entry indexed under the name of James McNichol, the missing Daniel's cousin. There was a brief note that the cousin had received news about Daniel from an unnamed person who claimed to have spoken to him.

This was something Bill Belshaw found intriguing. It opened up possibilities and gave him scope for investigation. But all of it would have to go back twenty-one months if he wasn't wasting his time on the wrong man.

He asked Mrs. McNichol, who now lived in a different part of Philadelphia, to undertake a gruesome and most unpleasant task. Tearfully she agreed. She travelled with Belshaw to the morgue, where she was shown the blue worsted suit Dr. Wadsworth had done his best to clean.

Lifting it to her face, her hand suddenly dropped.

"Yes," she said huskily, "it's Dan's."

Belshaw produced the crucifix.

"Dan's," she said.

Then the prayer-book.

"Dan's." She was close to collapse, but she held herself rigid until Belshaw had.told her the name of the tailor in Walnut Street. "Dan's tailor," she said in a whisper before yielding to a torrent of tears.

Bill Belshaw didn't feel elated at having provided himself with a short cut in his investigation. He was an experienced detective in a city that required its police to be experienced. The City of Brotherly Love from time to time produces some unlovely brethren who are capable of quite unbrotherly emotions.

But he wanted the story she could tell him. Much would depend on where it led.

A young woman drained of emotion, who had no more tears to shed, told Belshaw of her marriage to a man she loved and of their happiness in sharing their new home. They had no secrets, their enthusiasms and ambitions were shared. Marie McNichol had been a happy wife who expected to become a happy mother, for she was aware she was carrying the child of the man she loved.

Then one day Dan McNichol went to work and did not return. His partner seemed as surprised as she at McNichol's disappearance.

When several days had gone by she got in touch with her husband's family. They had heard nothing and advised her to go to the police. She had rung up the police station and had then gone and made a statement.

But some months later she had informed the police there was no reason to continue making inquiries for her husband. His partner had run into him in New York. So she knew he was alive.

"Did your husband get on well with Keller?" Belshaw asked.

"They were partners." She shook her head. "I don't think Dan was terribly fond of Keller, but then you don't have to be fond of a business partner, do you?"

"Has Keller seen your husband since that first time in New York?"

She nodded, but it seemed she did so reluctantly to the watchful police lieutenant.

"Yes," she said, "there was another occasion, but it was not after the other occasion. It was before it. You see, I was staying with my mother, and Keller called at our home to tell me Dan was here in Philadelphia."

"He had seen him?"

"I suppose so, yes."

"Why did he call at your home?"

"I learned later it was because he had a message from Dan. My husband wanted help."

"What kind?"

Mrs. McNichol's face worked as though she was once more about to break down under the strain, but again she overcame her obvious distress and said, "Dan had become a tramp. He was down and out, lieutenant, and ashamed to face me. He needed money and clothes. Keller told me he had been out on the road, and was now practically destitute."

"What did you do?" Belshaw asked.

"I packed up some of Dan's clothes that were still in the wardrobe, and gave them with some money to Keller, who assured me he'd be seeing my husband again. I told him to tell Dan to get himself fixed and then come home. He'd find me waiting just as though nothing had happened."

"But he didn't come home?"

"No, lieutenant," said the woman unhappily. "I waited,

but I didn't hear his key in the lock. So I went to see Keller. He told me he had given the clothes and money and my message to Dan and had arranged to meet him again. But my husband didn't keep the appointment and Keller lost contact with him."

As Belshaw was aware, with one partner absent, there still remained the leather business. But according to Mrs. Mc-Nichol her husband's partner had told her it was in debt and there was no way of pulling it out of the red. In fact, it was unwillingness to face up to bad debts that had probably sent Dan McNichol running from his home, his work, and anything that looked like being part of the general problem of day-to-day living.

"You think your husband had a breakdown, Mrs. Mc-Nichol?" Belshaw asked the woman.

"If he did he gave no sign of it before he left home that morning in March last year," she said, her chin lifting a trifle defiantly.

Belshaw believed her.

As soon as she had gone home he started a fresh inquiry. This time he wanted to find Edward Keller. The dead man's partner had been evasive, in Belshaw's opinion. There were a number of questions he could answer. Especially about his meetings with Dan McNichol who had become a tramp and had been seen in New York.

Almost the first thing he turned up about Keller was that, in the very month McNichol had left home to disappear, when the Red Star Laundry was functioning shortly before it closed, it was run by two partners. Edward J. Connery and Edward Keller. Just as the leather business of McNichol and Keller had run into debt, so the laundry business of Connery and Keller ran into bankruptcy.

Edward Keller could be said to operate under a dark star more certainly than a red one.

Probing away, Belshaw learned that Connery, fed up, had cleared out of Philadelphia and gone north to New Jersey.

Keller had a different way of solving his problems. He had gone no farther than his home in Frankford Avenue, where he sank in a chair and let his wife go out to work and decide if she was better at providing for the family than her husband.

Belshaw told one of his plain-clothes men to keep watch on the house, informing headquarters by phone of any move Keller made. Before the first report came he was told, "There's a Mrs. Keller wants to talk to you, lieutenant."

Belshaw didn't pretend he wasn't surprised by this move, whatever it portended. He had the phone call switched through and a woman's voice said crisply, "That Lieutenant Belshaw who's investigating this corpse found in the laundry? Well, my husband asked me to give you a message, lieutenant. He's gone to the Madison Street factory and will be there when you call."

Before Belshaw could ask a question the caller rang off. He felt annoyed, and he knew the reports in the newspapers of the finding of the trunk at the empty laundry was responsible for Keller having time to think up some fresh moves to keep ahead of the police. He went to Madison Street. He found the factory and he found Keller, sitting in the front office.

For Belshaw's part, it was dislike at first sight. He never trusted a man whose face didn't balance. Edward Keller had a face composed of different halves. The right side looked like the face of a human wolf. Even the right eye had a gleam that the Philadelphia detective later called malicious. The left side of the face was that of a pious, timid man. "It negatived one's suspicions," was how Belshaw described it. Of the face as a whole he said, "It was one of the most marked cases of dual physiognomy I have ever seen." And Bill Belshaw was much more observant than the average man with his share of human curiosity.

Keller, as he had suspected, was prepared for the visit, and for the questions Belshaw had brought with him. But it did nothing to help Belshaw's temper that the other man took no trouble to mask his contempt for his visitor.

Suddenly Belshaw stopped asking questions. He knew he was getting nowhere and only shock tactics might work a change that could be helpful.

"All right, on your feet, Keller," he said.

That produced a change, he had to admit.

"What the hell's this?" Keller demanded, pushing back his chair and rising.

"You're coming down to headquarters. We'll finish this talk there. It's where folk like you, Keller, get co-operative. Fast."

"Now look here, lieutenant——"

But Belshaw wasn't bluffing. "Grab your hat and let's go," he said.

At Philadelphia police headquarters Belshaw and his men kept up a steady stream of questions, but Keller didn't crack under pressure. He didn't get panicky and shout for a lawyer, he didn't trick himself with a provable lie. He just sat there and sweated it out, hour after hour, keeping to his tale, telling it over and over, coming back to individual points and repeating them *ad nauseam*.

It was a performance that earned Belshaw's grudging respect. Keller didn't look tough, but he did look mean. He was both and in about equal measure. That made him truly formidable.

He claimed that he had grown tired of the leather business and its piling debts and had wound up the partnership with Dan McNichol in April 1914. That is, a month after the date on the police blotter, and of course if this were true it helped to put Keller in the clear so far as being concerned in a possible murder.

He added that he had another project lined up, the Red Star Laundry. He went into that with Ed Connery, whom he had known some time and liked. But the venture ran into bad luck.

The last occasion he had seen McNichol was the previous October, and that was when his ex-partner had asked him to call on Mrs. McNichol. She had been staying with her mother on the other side of town, and he hadn't seen her when he called at the house where she had lived with her husband. When he did see her he passed on Dan's message and asked her for some of his clothes and any cash she could spare. He took the clothes and money, kept an appointment he had made with Dan, handed over what he had received from Mrs. McNichol, and had watched the husband walk off. That was the last time he had seen him.

There was the little detail of the trunk found in the empty laundry, but he knew nothing about it, and he kept saying so every time he was asked.

Of course, if he had told the truth, if the clothes and money had been passed to Dan McNichol in October, then the corpse in the laundry was not McNichol's according to Dr. Wadsworth's medical testimony.

But Belshaw was convinced Keller was lying. He took a chance and held him in custody. As he couldn't do that for more than twenty-four hours, next day he brought a charge. Keller was arrested for murder, and Bill Belshaw was really on his mettle. He knew then this was the big case of his career, one that could make him or break him as a cop who rated. His neck was stuck way out.

James McNichol told him that when his cousin Dan left college he wanted to go into business, but after he started up with Keller Dan McNichol had quickly disagreed with the other's business methods, and there had been arguments and hard words between the partners. Keller, when questioned, had claimed he had never quarrelled with his former partner. But the cousin also told Belshaw that, like the wife, he had heard from Keller about Dan's disappearance. Keller had told him Dan had gone to the West Coast and the family would be having word from him before long.

James McNichol also mentioned Al Young, Keller's nephew from New York, who had been staying with his uncle at the time Dan McNichol vanished.

Belshaw pulled every string offered his hands by the Philadelphia police department, and they were many, but he never found Al Young. The nephew of Edward Keller had apparently vanished with the same mysterious skill as his ex-partner. Belshaw was left contemplating the possibility that Keller had not only rid himself of a partner who was an encumbrance and perhaps a liability, but also a nephew who had helped him to dispose of the partner's body, and so had become another encumbrance and an even greater liability.

Ex-partner Ed Connery couldn't offer much enlightenment. But he remembered an incident that might have significance, Belshaw thought. He had thought the laundry cellar a damp unpleasant hole. One day he had gone down to find Keller, and had almost reached the bottom step when the other man rose from a kneeling position in the darkness on the far side of the cellar and ran towards him.

"I'll be up in a few minutes. Go back, Ed," he had insisted.

Connery had time to glimpse the shovel in Keller's hand and a look of tension on his face, then he turned and went back up the stairs. Later Keller apologized for seeming on edge, and the incident had passed over and been forgotten in the negotiations for ending the laundry venture.

Independent witnesses told Belshaw that Dan McNichol around the time of his disappearance carried a gold watch and a sizeable sum in cash, for he had been thinking of paying off a mortgage loan. A tailor named Lipshutz checked that he had made the blue worsted suit for McNichol and a dentist named Moratta checked that the fillings in the corpse's teeth coincided with work he had done for the missing man. A pawnbroker named Rosenthal had loaned ten dollars on a gold watch with the number of Dan McNichol's. That was on April 17th, 1914. J. McNamee was the name of the man pledging the watch and the address he had given was 826 Wensley Street. Belshaw went to the house and wasn't surprised that the name McNamee meant nothing there. Nor was he surprised when he checked that Keller had once rented an apartment at 1818 in the same street, but no one living in the house remembered him.

So Belshaw had done a lot of work that confirmed his theory of Dan McNichol being murdered and his body dumped in the trunk found in the empty laundry, but he had come no closer to proving Keller was the murderer.

He had inquiries made along both sides of Wensley Street, and that was how he came to find Annie Seasman, who lived in a room at 1834.

Belshaw deserved a lucky break and Annie Seasman provided it when she told him of tearing her dress one day on a large packing case outside 1818, and being so angry she intended to complain to Mrs. Keller about the crate being left on the sidewalk. But when a day or so later she arrived at 1818 it was to learn the Kellers had moved. She had naturally supposed the crate was for their moveables.

The hard-working Philadelphia detective was encouraged to make fresh efforts to try to trace the sale of such a packing case. Every dealer in the city was contacted, and it was a man named Fendelman who recalled selling such a crate to two men. The elder had called the younger Al.

"Who was this older man?" Belshaw asked him.

"I don't know his name, but I had dealt with him before and I remember he was from a leather firm. I can check the address if you like."

"I'd like very much," Belshaw said grimly.

It was the premises in Hamilton Street.

It now seemed to the detective that Dan McNichol could have been murdered in Hamilton Street, the corpse brought to Wensley Street and packed in the trunk, which was secured in the crate and then taken to the laundry cellar.

Belshaw's case was almost complete, but he decided to find Al Young's mother, who was Keller's sister. She told him she hadn't seen her son for two years or heard from him since he went to visit his uncle. She also told Belshaw that Keller had once been in trouble, as she put it, with the police in New York. He had been sent to Sing-Sing. When he came out he changed his name from Keilblock to Keller.

Edward Keilblock, according to his police record, had served fourteen years in jail. That meant Edward Keller was an old lag of considerable experience. When checked it included embezzlement and burglary.

Back in Philadelphia, Belshaw visited Keller, told the man what he had uncovered.

"That don't mean I'm a murderer," Keller said, grinning back at the detective.

"You'd save a lot of trouble by making a fresh statement and confessing," Belshaw informed him.

"I can't save anybody trouble, lieutenant," Keller said insolently. "Only you can do that. Go out West and find Mc-Nichol."

One thing Belshaw's grim hunt had not produced was the thirty-two gun that had put a bullet in the laundry corpse. If he could have found it or even prove that Keller had ever been in possession of such a weapon his case would have been open and shut, in police parlance.

But Edward Keller came up for trial without that important item being handed over as an exhibit to the prosecution, and the defence made great capital out of the fact that there was no evidence pointing to the prisoner ever possessing such a weapon. Moreover, Keller adopted a firm line on the tricky subject of Al Young.

"Find Dan McNichol," he said, "and he'll tell you what happened to Al."

Mrs. Keller did her best to support her husband's claims, and she did her best to confuse the jury by agreeing that there was such a trunk as the one found in the laundry, and she remembered seeing it in the Wensley Street house. But it had disappeared with Al Young.

Edward Keller's defence was sufficiently staunch to have a possible murder verdict reduced to one of voluntary manslaughter. The prisoner was sentenced to from ten to twelve years in the Eastern State Penitentiary.

By that time Keller's grin was beginning to look somewhat strained.

He served eight years of the sentence and was released on parole in 1924, ten years after Dan McNichol was shot and pushed into a leather trunk. He would most likely have passed into complete oblivion except for an amazing coincidence that caps any other recounted in the previous pages.

In jail he worked as a craftsman making leather goods, and when he walked through the gates a free man he had about six thousand dollars in his pocket. He had one thought, to marry a woman who had visited him. Her name was Jenny Flanagan, and he had told her the woman calling herself Mrs. Keller was not really his wife. The pair appeared before a justice of the peace and he duly pronounced them man and wife. The newly-weds were met by reporters, who were hoping for a scoop and a revelation about a case that was eight years old but still remembered and even debated in Philadelphia. The new Mrs. Keller brightly told the men with their pencils poised that she had felt sorry for Ed. Well, he always had been something of a spellbinder with words. The pencils remained poised as the reporters looked at Keller. He started to talk. He was still talking about the great wrong he had suffered when the reporters began to drift away. They didn't need pencils and notebooks to report something that would be lost on the back page if the news editor thought it merited a mention.

There were no revelations, no news scoop.

Keller procured a watchman's job at a bank and for a little over a year he lay low biding his time. Then he made his biggest bid for fortune. Five days before Christmas in 1925 he stole twenty thousand dollars of late deposits and returned to his lodging, where he packed a couple of bags before crossing the city to take a room at the Lorraine Hotel. When he arrived he locked himself in, but couldn't sleep. In these days he might have procured a sedative, but forty years ago instant sleep could not be purchased across a counter. Another world war had to be waged before the instant age dawned.

The sleepless Keller repacked his bags, settled his bill although he had only been in the hotel an hour, and caught a taxi.

"Germantown and Chelten," he told the driver, naming a corner where two large thoroughfares met.

It was late and cranks were abroad, so the driver offered no words because a man with bags was going to a deserted street corner. That was his business.

The taxi arrived, and the driver turned to his fare and suddenly caught his breath. Keller was on the floor of the taxi, with banknotes decorating the mat and seat like giant confetti. He was taken to hospital where an examination established he had had a heart attack.

The man who came from police headquarters to collect a formal statement took a look at the face under the sheet and started.

"I can identify him," he told the doctor grimly.

So it was Bill Belshaw who signed one of the forms that enabled Edward Keller to pass neatly and tidily into the annals of crime.